Oxford Junior History **1**

THE INVADERS

D1424389

Roy Burrell

Oxford University Press by arrangement with the British Broadcasting Corporation

MORRISON'S ACADEMY

SESSION	NAME	FORM
19 -19	Alan Torgersen	P3
1991 -1992	Helen McPhee	P3
1992 -1993	Natalie	P3
19 -19		
19 -19		

First published 1980
Reprinted 1981 (twice), 1982, 1983

ISBN 0 19 918119 5

Oxford University Press, Walton Street, Oxford OX2 6DP

Oxford London Glasgow
New York Toronto Melbourne Auckland
Kuala Lumpur Singapore Hong Kong Tokyo
Delhi Bombay Calcutta Madras Karachi
Nairobi Dar es Salaam Cape Town

and associated companies in
Beirut Berlin Ibadan Mexico City Nicosia

Oxford is a trade mark of Oxford University Press

Typesetting by Tradespools Ltd., Frome, Somerset
Printed in Hong Kong

Contents

Chapter One   The Celts

1 The People

Have you ever been to London Airport? It is hard to imagine what this busy, bustling place with its roaring airliners has to do with history. Yet, many centuries ago, long before aeroplanes had been invented, Heathrow was a quiet country area.

During the Second World War, something was found there which showed that Heathrow had an interesting past. It was a Royal Air Force station in those days and needed a longer runway. Bulldozers scraped away the grass and soil and as they did, a strange pattern appeared.

There were lots of little dark circles in the lighter earth. Men from the museum came to look at them. They said that the circles had once been holes in which wooden posts had stood.

Everyone wanted to know how old they were and what they were for. The airmen were surprised when they were told.

'There was once a wooden building here,' said one of the museum men. 'It was most likely a temple and could have been put up more than 2,000 years ago.'

'Can holes tell you that?' asked an airman.

'Yes. The shape of the building is shown by where the holes are. We know that the holes had big posts in them. From this we think we know what the building was. Pieces of pottery can also help us to put it in the right period. If no one touches a spot where a hole has been dug, the signs of its position and shape will stay there almost for ever. You could dig a pit in your garden, fill it in, and thousands of years in the future someone could find it and even say how deep it had once been.'

'Who made the holes?' asked the airman.

Iron Age horse harness

Iron Age pottery

'We think it was the work of the Celts, who lived all over Britain in those days. They lived in Europe too, and wherever they settled, they left things which tell us something about them.'

The museum man was right. There was once a whole Celtic village near the temple and remains of the Celts are to be seen almost anywhere in Britain.

Sometimes there are simple finds like those above from Essex.

A lot of the remains are surprisingly large and much too big to put in a museum.

The Celts were noisy and quarrelsome according to their neighbours, the Romans. This is why they were nearly always fighting each other. When the Celts came to Britain, there was plenty of land available, even if the people who owned it had to be driven out first.

The earliest Celts in Britain made themselves villages of little round huts. Later on, when there was not enough land to go round, they began to fight amongst themselves.

Villages were started on islands, in lakes and marshes, on tongues of land sticking out into the sea, or on the tops of hills. The villagers would have felt safer behind the stronger defences of a hill fort. There are still scores of these to be seen in Britain.

above Remains of an Iron Age hill fort at Morvah in Cornwall
below The village at Heathrow

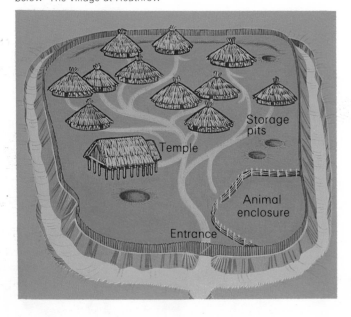

Storage pits

Temple

Animal enclosure

Entrance

2 A Hill Fort

Whenever a tribe went hungry, there were always men who would try to talk the others into moving to a new home. Sometimes they had their way, and the tribe went off, taking their animals and seed corn with them.

The warriors rode in their war chariots and behind them came flocks of sheep, herds of cattle and ox waggons laden with all that the tribe owned. Those with no carts had to walk.

When they came to a place they liked, they would try to drive out the people who lived there. If they managed to do this, they were lucky. If not, they had to move on.

Some tribes crossed from France to England in boats. Wherever they went, they found people already living. Land was not easy to capture. They did not always have the chance to strike the first blow. Often, the

Model of a chariot from Llyn Cerrig Bach in Wales

attack came from the owners of the land through which they were passing. The warriors would put on their helmets and take up their shields, swords and spears.

When both sides were ready, they whipped up their horses and drove their chariots towards each other. They hurled their spears and then jumped down to fight on foot. The rest of the newcomers watched from the ox waggons.

If the newcomers lost, they tried to get away as fast as they could. It wasn't always easy after this sort of battle.

Attacking a hill fort might be a simple matter if those who lived there had not kept the defences in repair. All the same, the invading warriors had to run uphill, while the defenders could hide behind the banks of earth and only show themselves to hurl stones.

The attackers could shelter behind their shields but they found it much harder to fight up a slope. Those at the top of the hill had no trouble in throwing stones downwards.

Almost 2,000 years ago a wandering Celtic tribe made war on the people who lived in Maiden Castle. This huge hill fort is in the West Country. At that time its defences were not as strong as they should have been.

The Celts were too impatient to camp round the hill and wait for those inside to run out of food and water. They moved towards the fort and were met with a hail of stones which most of them managed to take on their shields.

After a while, there were fewer stones because the men inside had been too lazy to collect enough. The leader of the attackers shouted to his men to move faster. They ran up the slopes and a lot of them climbed over the walls and into the ditches where they fought with their swords.

As soon as they had cleared the first ditch, they scrambled up to the next one and then the one beyond that. Finally they came out on the flat top of the hill and there was little more fighting.

The chief told everyone what to do so that the fortress would not be taken so easily the next time. The ditches would have to be made deeper, more stones must be added to the walls and new posts cut to stop them sliding down the hillside. The huts on the hilltop had to be tackled next. A few could be used but most had to be rebuilt. While this was going on, the farmers were sent to take over the fields in the lowlands.

When the repairs had been completed, sacrifices were made to the gods. They hoped that the gods would help them when their new home was next attacked.

3 The Family

Imagine that it is now ten years since the Celtic tribe captured Maiden Castle and they have settled down a little. They still go on raids for cattle from time to time but there are no more full-scale wars. The warriors practise with their weapons. The craftsmen make things and the farmers grow food.

Let us visit a farm. The children live in the round farmhouse. They sleep on springy piles of heather or bracken laid on the hard dirt floor. Their parents' bed is a pair of wooden benches draped with sheep skins.

The children don't wear pyjamas or nightdresses. If it is very cold, they keep their

day clothes on and snuggle under sheep skins, but most nights they pull off their clothes before they lie down to sleep. The house is usually warm because the fire is never allowed to go out.

A little while after the sun has risen, Briacan wakes up. He is thirteen. He pulls on his long trousers and wakes his younger brother, Awyl, who is ten. Awyl yawns and goes with Briacan to fetch wood for the fire. He will dress later.

The fresh air from the open door wakens their sister, Clawen, who is eight. She puts on her blouse and skirt and is surprised to find her parents are still asleep. Usually Baban, the baby, wakes everyone up.

'*Does Baban always cry in the mornings?*' we ask Briacan when he and Awyl come back with the wood for the fire.

'No, not always. Mother is often the first to wake. Then Clawen goes to get water from the spring.'

'*What do you do all day?*'

'Well, we don't have much time for playing because we have to help our parents. Clawen has to do what Mother tells her. She seems to like looking after the baby best.

'She also has to get Grandmother her food. Granny is too old to move about much. She sleeps with my two aunts in a space at the back of our round house.'

When Clawen comes back with the water, everyone is up and even Awyl is dressed. No one washes unless they are very dirty. Everyone sits to eat the oat cakes mother has cooked and Briacan wants to know what he must do today. Father brushes crumbs from his long, reddish moustache and thinks.

'We have finished the ploughing,' he says, 'and now the sheep must be brought to the top field for shearing.' The boys like this. If they can get the sheep in quickly, there will be time for games.

left Bronze dish
above Iron Age pottery from Maiden Castle

9

4 The Children

It takes all the morning to collect the sheep. Then they eat the dark bread and goat's cheese mother has given them. They wash it down with weak beer from a goatskin. After a rest they will play. They have to make the toys they need.

Briacan sharpens both ends of a short piece of wood and lays it on the grass. He tries to hit one of the sharp tips with the butt of his spear. The 'rat', as they call it, will fly away if he gets it just right.

'Do you have any other games, Briacan?'

'I like our next game best. Last year one of us used the spear to bat away a stone thrown by the other. Awyl missed and the stone hit him instead. So I had an idea. We collected tufts of wool from gorse bushes, twisted them into a long thread and wound it round the stone. The ball was much better. In fact it was too good. It bounced and rolled so much that we lost it.'

It is very warm for springtime, so the boys have a splash in a nearby pond. While they are drying off in the sun, they play 'knife-cloth-stone'. On the count of three, each player brings his hand out from behind his back. One pointing finger is a knife, a fist is a stone and a flat hand a cloth.

A knife beats cloth because it can cut cloth, but loses to the stone which can blunt it. Cloth is better than stone because it can wrap round the stone. Before long they argue over

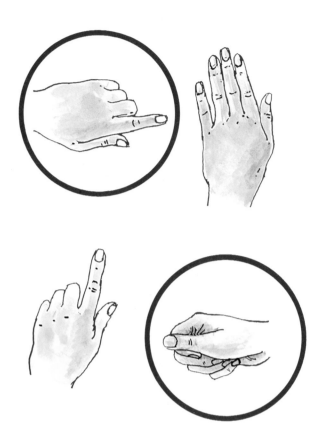

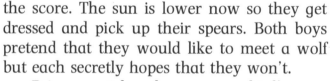

the score. The sun is lower now so they get dressed and pick up their spears. Both boys pretend that they would like to meet a wolf but each secretly hopes that they won't.

Briacan wishes he was a chief's son, learning to fight with real weapons and driving a chariot. Then he would not have to go with the other children collecting mushrooms and berries or gathering the seeds of wild plants for making into porridge. He wouldn't have to work on the farm either.

When they get back, Clawen tells them that she is learning to weave. She can cook already. Grandmother and her aunts show her what to do whenever they have time.

5 The Tribe

The king and his warriors practised chariot driving and different kinds of fighting. They were interested in breeding and training horses but they left the care of the other animals, such as sheep and cows, to those who did not fight. Because they kept the rest of the tribe safe from its enemies, they expected the farmers to work hard and grow extra food to feed them.

Briacan's father is a farmer who has only a few small fields. Some of his father's friends have farms so big they have to have slaves to do the work. There were many different kinds of jobs which had to be done throughout the year.

Briacan's mother looks after the children, gets the meals ready and makes the clothes from thread which she has spun herself.

Every grown-up had to be able to earn a

living by doing these simple tasks. People with special skills were looked up to by the others. They were the craftsmen of the tribe. They spent most of their time doing the one thing they were good at.

In every tribe the blacksmith is the leading craftsman.

'*Why is your job so important?*' we ask him.

'Because we are a tribe of warriors,' he answers proudly. 'We Celts have won a lot of battles with our iron swords. Many of our enemies have to make do with bronze ones. Bronze is not as good as iron and much harder to get.

'I don't just forge good swords. I also make spear and arrow heads as well as other things.

'When we find the iron, it is mixed in with rock and has to be dug out of the ground in lumps. It is called iron ore. The ore is brought to the smithy where I heat it in a fire. My helpers blow air into the fire with bellows to make it hotter.

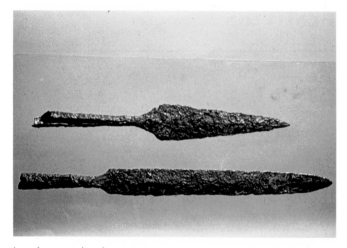

Iron Age spearheads

'I grip a glowing lump with my tongs, lay it on the anvil and hammer it. Specks of hot rock fly away in showers of golden sparks. When most of the rock has gone, I put the iron that is left back in the fire. After a while it's soft enough to be taken out again. I beat it out on my anvil into the shape I want. A tribe is as good as its weapons and that's why we smiths are so important.'

6 Festivals

Let's ask Briacan about the holidays he has.

'Holidays? What are holidays?'

'*When you don't go to school or do any work,*' we explain.

'Oh, I see. You mean *holy* days. I don't know what you mean by school, but we do have festivals four times a year when work stops.'

'*Like our Easter, Whitsun and Christmas?*'

'I don't know what they are. We call our festivals Samhain, Imbolg, Beltane and Lugnasa. Samhain is the most important. It comes in the late autumn and really marks the start of winter. It's the first feast of the year.'

The Celts were mostly farmers and warriors. When the crops failed or the cows fell ill, they did not know why. They thought that someone had cast a spell, or more likely, that the gods were angry. They held feasts throughout the year to please the gods and put them in a good mood.

They held great religious services in honour of the 'Other-world', as they called the place where the dead went and the gods lived. They made sacrifices both of animals and human beings. The chants and prayers had to be said in exactly the right way or they thought their plants would not grow in the fields and the animals would give no milk or even die.

The Celts didn't know about the germs which were the most likely cause of these things so they tried magic. Most of us don't really believe in magic, although we would like to. When you have been in trouble, have you ever said to yourself, '*If I touch every lamp post on the way to school, I won't be punished*'?

You know in your secret heart that it doesn't work but you've got to do all you can. The Celts knew that they couldn't do much about disasters, so perhaps magic was the answer.

Every three months there was a festival. Samhain came on the first of November and marked not only the onset of winter but also the beginning of the Celtic new year.

The magic rites started the evening before. They were meant to protect the people and bring them good luck. It was the time when the Other-world spirits could be seen by ordinary folk and this could be dangerous, as the following story shows.

Wooden idol from Dagenham

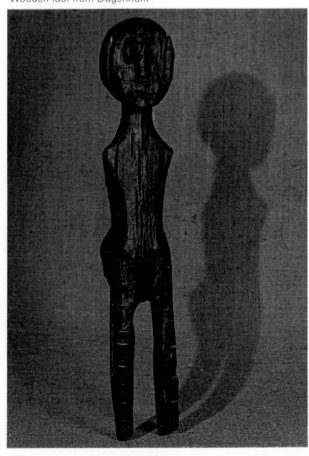

On the Eve of Samhain one year, a handsome stranger came to the village and asked to meet the best harpist in the area, a man named Culag. The stranger offered Culag a bag of gold if he would come and play at a feast. At first Culag refused but a sight of the gold tempted him and at last he went with the stranger to a large hall not far away where there were over a hundred guests. Culag played music for them all night until he became so tired, he fell asleep.

When he awoke the next morning, he found himself lying on the grass at the foot of a little hill near a small lake. He was still clutching his harp and the leather purse he had been given. Alas! There were only stones in it.

As he stumbled to his feet, he caught sight of his reflection in the lake. He was amazed at the face which stared back at him. The skin was wrinkled and both his hair and beard were long, tangled and snow-white. When he got home, he found that thirty years had passed. His wife had died and his children were grown and did not know him.

The story of Culag was told to the children as an awful warning of what could happen on the Eve of Samhain. Memories of the festival of Samhain have come down to us through the ages. Today we know it as Hallowe'en.

By the first of February, the earliest flowers were in bloom and the young lambs were being born. Sheep were very important to the Celts because their wool was needed to make clothes. February the first was called Imbolg. The goddess of the feast was Brigit. People prayed to her and made sacrifices on her altars. By doing this, they were hoping that she would give them large and healthy flocks.

15

7 Beltane and Lugnasa

Three months later came Beltane which was held on the first of May. The name may have come from the god Belenos, or it may mean 'bright fire'. It was yet another chance for the Celts to pray to the Other-world to send them luck and riches. Two huge bonfires were lit and the cattle were driven through the flames to make them clean and pure. In many parts of Europe, including Scotland and Ireland, the custom of May Day bonfires survived until modern times.

The last period of the year started on August the first. Its name was Lugnasa and it went on longer than the other festivals. The day of Lugnasa came in the middle of a month of feasting and merry-making. It was in honour of the god Lugus. There were often sports, fairs, games and 'pretend' fights.

It was a custom to hold an enormous get-together to which all the people of an area were invited. It was the one time in the year when people could enjoy themselves with their relations and friends.

Chris Molan

16

8 The Druids

All the festivals were run by the Druids. These were the priests of the tribe and only the king came above them. Sometimes they lived away from the tribe in holy places in the forests. They held ceremonies in clearings in the forest, particularly where there were oak trees. The oak was believed to be a holy tree and so was the mistletoe which grows on it. The Druids thought mistletoe was a powerful medicine. The Roman writer Pliny describes how they gathered it.

'The mistletoe is rarely found, but when it is, the Druids gather it with solemn ceremony. They do this on the sixth day of their first month. After the preparations have been made for the sacrifice or feast under the tree, they bring two white bulls. A priest dressed in a white robe climbs the tree and cuts the mistletoe with a golden sickle. The plant is caught in a white cloth. Then they sacrifice the victims and pray to their gods for good luck. They believe that a potion made from mistletoe is a remedy against all poison.'

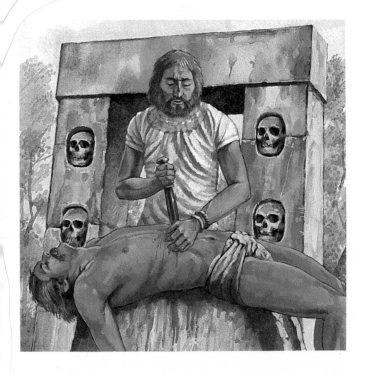

The Druids were medicine men and magicians. Woe betide anyone who annoyed a Druid. A spell said properly could ruin his crops or stop his cows giving milk. If the Druid were really cross he might curse the man until he died.

Druids did not fight but they sometimes went to a battle to put spells on the attackers. If an enemy were frightened enough, he would be easier to beat.

Even when there were no wars, a man might quarrel with his neighbour, perhaps about the boundary between their farms. The Druid would decide who was right and that was an end of the matter.

A few Druids could read and write but none of them really trusted books – they preferred to keep everything they had to know in their heads. They started their training as boys and were taught by an older man. They sat on the floor of his hut and listened as he recited the piece for that day. It might be a spell, a family tree or a list of laws. The teacher said a line and the class repeated it after him. They went on doing this until they knew the piece by heart. They had no need of pencils, exercise books or satchels.

Some tribes had a wise man or woman who could tell what was going to happen in the future. If the king wanted to know whether he should fight against another tribe, he would ask the Druid. An animal, or even a human being, would be sacrificed. The body was then laid out and the Druid looked at it carefully. The Celts believed that he was able to see things which had not yet happened by doing this.

The Celts thought nothing of sacrificing a captured enemy so that they would know if it was to be a lucky day for them. They might burn him to death or cut off his head. The heads were sacred and kept in a shrine in the forest. Sometimes a clever carver made a full-sized model of one of these heads, either in wood or in stone. Here are pictures of these statues. The word Druid may mean 'wise man of the oak trees', so it isn't surprising to find that the wooden statues are nearly always made of oak.

Druids' shrine from France; stone head from Gloucester

Work Section

Understand your Work

1 The People
1 What is an archaeologist?
2 Where is London airport?
3 How can a pattern of holes in the ground show what shape a building was?
4 How do we know what sort of people the Celts were?
5 Where in Britain might Celtic remains be found?
6 Were there already people living in Britain when the Celts invaded?
7 Why did the Celts choose to build villages in the following areas: a) lakes; b) hilltops; c) tongues of land sticking out into the sea?
8 Are there many Celtic forts in Britain?
9 Describe one of the objects in the photographs on page 5 and say what it might have been used for.
10 What sort of Celtic remains are too big to go in museums?

2 A Hill Fort
1 Why might a tribe go hungry?
2 How did the people of the tribe move their belongings?
3 What sort of weapons were used?
4 Where is Maiden Castle? Can you find it on a map?
5 What size and shape of stone is best for throwing at an attacker?
6 How long ago did the battle take place?
7 Why were the farmers' fields outside the Castle?
8 How and why did the victors sacrifice to the gods?
9 Describe what is happening in the picture on pages 6 and 7.
10 What does the photograph on page 6 show?

3 The Family
1 The names of the children, as well as the children themselves, are imaginary. Why could we not use real names?
2 How are the children's sleeping arrangements different from your own?
3 Where do the children get wood and water?
4 Why do you think the fire is never allowed to go out?
5 How might a fire be lit?
6 Is Briacan's father a warrior, a craftsman or a farmer?
7 How many people live in the hut?
8 Where do you think the family gets its clothes?
9 Describe the breakfast scene on page 9.
10 How are the pots in the photographs on page 9 different from those you use at home?

4 The Children
1 Why do the boys have to collect the sheep?
2 What will happen to the wool?
3 Do the children's parents buy toys for them?
4 What sorts of food and drink are mentioned?
5 Is all the food grown on the farm?
6 What meals do you like that these children could not have had?
7 What games do you play that these children could not have known about?
8 Why should Clawen need to know how to weave?
9 What are the weights for in the picture on page 11?
10 Describe the cloth that Clawen is weaving.

5 The Tribe
1 Would there be one king in Britain or many?
2 Would the tribes spend more time farming than fighting?
3 Why should the warriors be interested in breeding horses but not the other animals mentioned?
4 Why were the craftsmen of the tribe greatly respected?
5 Were all the farms the same size?
6 What is iron like when it is found? What is it called?
7 What sort of objects might a blacksmith make for the farmers?
8 Where did the pots, pans, knives and forks in your own home come from?
9 Describe the objects in the photograph on page 13.
10 Describe the jobs shown in the pictures on pages 12 and 13.

6 Festivals
1 Why doesn't Briacan know what a school is?
2 What is a festival?
3 Why has Briacan not heard of Easter, Whitsun and Christmas?
4 What was the Other-world? When could people from the Other-world be seen?
5 Was the Celtic new year at the same time as our own?
6 What did the Celts hope the magic rites would do?
7 What causes disease in cattle?
8 What do we do about sick farm animals?
9 What do you think had happened to Culag?
10 What, do you think, is the object in the photograph on page 14 and how might it have been used?

7 Beltane and Lugnasa
1 Where does the name Beltane come from?
2 How many Celtic gods and goddesses can you name?
3 Why did the Celts pray to the Other-world spirits?
4 Did any traces of the Beltane festival survive until modern times?
5 Look up hallowe'en in your dictionary. Do you think the date on which it falls has anything to do with Samhain?
6 What did the Celts do at Lugnasa?
7 What does 'superstition' mean?
8 Do we hold May Day celebrations today?
9 What is happening in the picture on pages 16 and 17?
10 Who seems to be in charge of what is happening?

8 The Druids
1 Who were the Druids?
2 Where did the Druids hold their ceremonies?
3 What did the Celts believe about mistletoe?
4 When did the Druids collect mistletoe?
5 When do we hang up mistletoe nowadays?
6 How did the Druids try to help their warriors?
7 How did the Druids learn their laws and spells?
8 How did the Druids try to foretell the future?
9 Describe what is happening in the picture on page 18.
10 What does the photograph on page 19 show?

Further Work

1 Make a model of a Celtic hut from twigs and dry grass. Your group might like to try and make a hill fort.
2 Draw a picture of a Celtic warrior. Study pictures of weapons and clothes before you make a start.
3 Try and visit your nearest hill fort. Make a plan of it.
4 How easy is it to learn things by heart? Try the following experiment. Find a short story or a long poem that you like. Each person in your group learns part of the poem or story by heart. You must read your part over and over again until you know it. When all the parts have been learned, the members of your group will be able to tell the whole story or poem. Is it easier to learn stories or poetry by heart?
5 You can still buy cheese made from the milk of goats and sheep at some supermarkets and shops. Try to get some and describe how its taste is different from the cheese you usually eat.
6 Describe and draw some of the Celtic objects in your nearest museum.
7 Try some of the games Briacan and Awyl play. You could make a ball by winding wool around a small stone.
8 How is your own home different from a Celtic one? Think about building materials, heating, cooking, water, furniture, eating, washing and sleeping.

Use your Imagination

1 Why have the Celts' homes and temples disappeared?
2 Why is it important for a tribe to own a lot of land?
3 Imagine you were a warrior during an attack on a hill fort. Describe what happened.
4 Write a speech for the Celtic chief. Give orders to your tribe for repairing the fort you have captured.
5 Imagine you are watching a sacrifice to the gods. Describe what takes place.
6 Imagine you are Awyl or Clawen. Describe how you spend your day.
7 Say why you think sheep are so important to the family.
8 The tribe's blacksmith is proud of his job. He tells us what an important man he is. Why are there so few blacksmiths today?
9 Why do you think the Celts didn't know about germs?
10 Why might some people like to believe in magic?
11 Imagine that you are one of Culag's children. Tell the story of your father's home-coming.
12 Some people today claim to be able to read the future. They don't make sacrifices in order to do this. What do they use? Can the future really be known? Would you want to know what is going to happen?

Chapter Two   The Romans

1 Fishbourne

No one lives in this house. No one wants to any more. The windows are broken. Tiles have slipped off the roof. The rain will soak the wooden beams until they rot and fall down. After a long while, the walls will crumble and there will be nothing left but a heap of bits and pieces.

Dust will blow across the heap and bury it. Weeds will grow so thickly that you would never know that a house once stood there. Because it is too much trouble to clear away the rubble, it will be left. A new house might be built on top of it or someone might find the remains hundreds of years later. If someone did not paint and repair the house you live in, the same thing could happen.

In 1960 a workman was digging a ditch in a field at Fishbourne, near Chichester in Sussex. He found some strange pieces of broken tile like these:

He called the foreman to come and look at them and asked him what they were. The foreman shook his head. 'I don't know,' he said. 'I've never seen anything like them before.' The workman said, 'They could be old. What should we do with them?' 'Perhaps we should take them to a museum,' the foreman replied.

Mrs. Rule, the lady from the museum, was very excited by the pieces of tile. She asked if she and her helpers might come and dig in the field. She thought that the pieces were most likely Roman and nearly 2,000 years old.

The diggers from the museum soon found the remains of a house. The wood and most of the plaster had rotted away. But there were enough tiles, bricks and stones for them to work out what it had once looked like. It turned out to be very large and must have belonged to someone very rich and important.

The house and all the objects were indeed Roman and many centuries old. The diggers

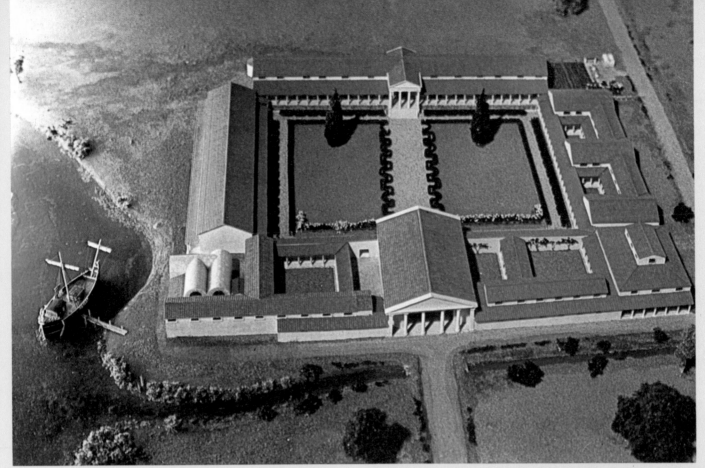

above A reconstruction of Fishbourne Palace

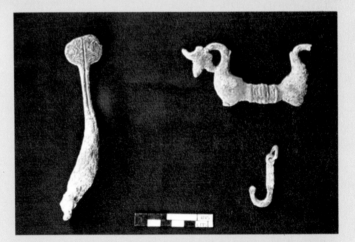

also found a great many everyday things. These have been put in a museum made specially to hold them. They tell us a lot about the way people lived in those days. Perhaps you can guess what they were.

2 The People

Julius Caesar

Claudius Caesar

What were the Romans doing in Britain? Why did they build the house at Fishbourne?

Rome is a town in Italy and had started as a village of mud huts nearly three thousand years ago.

The earliest Romans were farmers and shepherds. When they were raided, they hid in the hills around the village. To make themselves safer they built a wall round their hills. It's easier to fight your attacker if he is below you.

The Romans quickly learned that the best way of dealing with an enemy was to attack him before he could attack them. So they left their farms, took their weapons and raided the most dangerous of the nearby villages.

Before long, they had captured all the towns and villages in their area. They trained men to be full-time soldiers. Before this, the Romans had fought only when there was danger. Now, the full-time soldiers could conquer even more land. At last Rome ruled the whole of Italy. The Romans went on fighting until they owned all the land round the Mediterranean Sea.

One of the army leaders was called Julius Caesar. He conquered the land of Gaul which today we call France. Some of the prisoners he took in France were from Britain. So Julius Caesar made up his mind to find out what that country was like. He crossed the Channel twice but he did not conquer Britain. That was

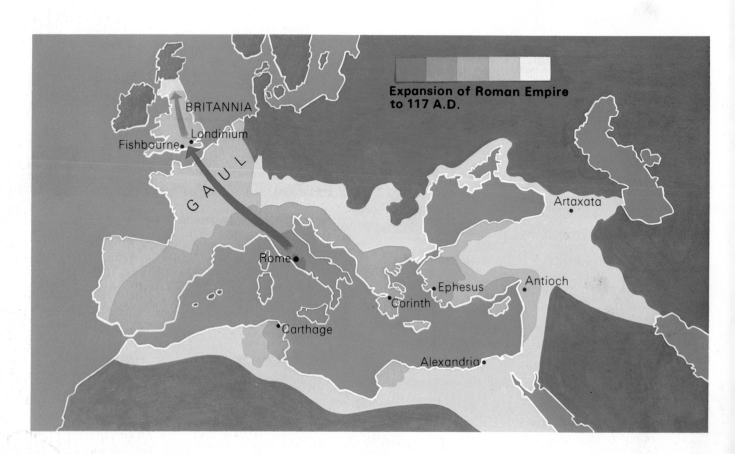

Expansion of Roman Empire to 117 A.D.

BRITANNIA
Londinium
Fishbourne
GAUL
Rome
Artaxata
Ephesus
Antioch
Corinth
Carthage
Alexandria

done by the armies of Claudius Caesar nearly a hundred years later.

The legions which Claudius sent here gradually pushed the Britons back. One by one the chiefs of the tribes gave in. But the Romans showed the beaten tribesmen how much better it was to live in towns and well-made houses. In a few years, Britain was dotted with towns and villas, as the large houses were called.

There were many reasons why the Romans came. They wanted corn, leather, wool, tin, copper, lead, gold, silver and slaves. They made sure that those who helped them to get these things were well paid. The house at Fishbourne was probably a reward given to one of their British friends. And perhaps they came to Britain because once you start conquering, it's hard to stop.

How Rome may have begun

The army of Claudius invades Britain

3 The Family

This picture shows excavations on the site of a Roman country house. Let's imagine what it looked like when the Romans were here. You can see into the bedroom of Marcus and his younger brother, Lucius. There is not much furniture, just two beds, a stool each and a chest for clothes.

The boys have to get up early. They go to school in the nearby town. They don't have much of a wash because they will bathe in the afternoon. They do this every weekday. You can see them putting on their tunics and sandals.

Look at the lavatory. It is next to the bathroom. The used bath water can flush the toilets. When the boys have washed their hands and faces, they go and meet their parents and their sister Julia in the dining room.

After breakfast, all three children must go off to school. Usually they have to walk but

Key to Roman Villa **1** main reception room **2** living room **3** boys' bedroom **4** cold bath **5** hot room **6** lavatory **7** smoke-stack of hot room furnace

this morning they can get a lift on a cart. Their mother's name is Marcia. She tells them to put on an extra cloak. The main part of the villa has central heating but outdoors thick clothes have to be worn.

School starts at eight o'clock and goes on until after midday. The fathers of the pupils have to pay the magister or teacher. Poor people can't afford to send their children to school after they are about eleven or twelve. It costs more then. More boys go to school than girls. Most girls stay at home to help their mothers.

below and right Roman tableware

27

4 School

There are only about ten pupils at the school. It is at the back of a shop in the town square. As you can see, it is rather bare. There are no charts or pictures on the walls. The lessons are mostly reading and writing, with a little arithmetic.

The children have to copy pieces from books by famous writers. The language they use is Latin. Paper and parchment are too dear so they use a little wooden board covered with wax. Each child writes with a sharp piece of wood. If he makes a mistake, he uses the other end of his pen to rub it out. You can see that the Romans didn't use our modern numbers. They find it hard to do sums with letters. They are doing arithmetic with pebbles and bead frames.

Roman writing materials

When Marcus, Lucius and Julia have finished their lessons, they put their things in their satchels and go home for the midday meal.

Father's friend, Maradus, is visiting and the two men lie on couches. The slaves bring in the cold meat, salad and sausages and later, pancakes with honey. The three grown-ups drink wine. The children drink a mixture of wine and water.

above Slave at work in a Roman kitchen
left Reconstruction of a kitchen in a Romano-British house

5 Making a Living

Father's name is Cornelius. He has to earn money to keep his family in comfort. He owns a large stretch of land around the villa. He is head of the family so no one argues with him. Cornelius runs the family business and sells things from the farms on his land. The farm work is done by slaves.

Cornelius is in charge of religion on the estate as well. Romans have many gods. Some of them are famous and important. Others are not so well known. There are gods to look after everything, even the house, the fields and the food stores. The villa has a small temple or shrine on the far side of the garden.

Let's ask Cornelius what the shrine is for.

'It's where I make my offerings of corn and wine to the gods. I must get their advice and blessing before anything is decided in the

Remains of the shrine at Lullingstone villa

family. I wouldn't plant my corn, start a journey or do a business deal until I'd been to pray at the shrine.'

owners got theirs free as a reward for serving in the army. Some owners rent their land to farmers; they say they don't have time to spare from their duties as town councillors. But Maradus and I prefer to run things personally. I manage to help run the town as well. I'm also a magistrate. At my court in the forum I hear cases and try to settle the townspeople's arguments.'

'*Does everyone do this?*'

'Most people do. In the family it's the father who is in charge of religion. My friend Maradus is a Briton who has learnt our ways but he isn't quite as careful about these things as a proper Roman would be. Mind you, he doesn't have to worry about Ceres, the goddess of harvests. The slaves at his villa don't grow crops, they make things out of clay.'

'*What things?*'

'Tiles and bricks for buildings; cups, beakers, bowls, jugs and jars for the kitchen and dining table. Maradus is lucky. He can tell his workers what to do in their own language but he speaks Latin almost like a Roman. He had to buy his land, although most villa

6 In the Town

In the afternoon, Cornelius has to go back to the town. Marcia is going with him and they will take the children as well. Marcia wants to get some material for making clothes. The house slaves do the everyday shopping. They buy most of the food from the market stalls. For special things, however, Marcia goes herself.

Stone carving of a Roman shop

Julia likes shopping too. The boys are being allowed to go to the gymnasium at the public baths where they can meet their friends and play games.

They will all meet in the forum afterwards.

Remains of Roman shops in Italy

Some soldiers are expected to arrive in an hour or two and everyone wants to be there when they come. The soldiers are part of a legion which has been sent to the town. One of the officers is Marcia's brother, Gaius. The children are looking forward to seeing their uncle again.

Cornelius joins his family just in time to see the officers ride into the square. These are followed by the legionaries on foot. An orderly leads Uncle Gaius's horse away and he is soon surrounded by the family. Everyone is laughing and talking at once. The ordinary soldiers are marched off to camp by the centurions.

Back at the villa everybody wants to hear what the news is from Rome. Gaius Julius Decuminus, to give him his full name, will take a bath after his long journey. Cornelius and the boys have not yet bathed today, so they will join him.

7 A Story

Marcus was told not to play with his uncle's sword. But he did, and that's how he cut his hand. 'Sit down Marcus,' says his father. 'I'm going to tell you a story.

'Once upon a time when the world was young, the gods moved about their business, keeping the earth a pleasant place to live in. Neptune ruled the seas, Diana lit the different faces of the moon and Phoebus drove his sun chariot across the sky every day.

'Phoebus was a magnificent god, dressed in gold and silver with a shining crown on his head. Few could look at him without being dazzled. Every morning his slaves decked him in all his finery whilst those in the coach-house cleaned and polished the chariot. The stable boys groomed the four strong and spirited horses, ready for the time when their master would take his place at the start of the day.

'And every morning, Phoebus drove the glittering team up the steep slope of the sky, bringing light, warmth and life to the people below.

'Phoebus had a son named Phaeton, whom he had never seen. Many times the boy had asked his mother to take him to meet his father but she had always refused. The journey to the east was far too long and difficult she said.

'The boys at his school jeered at Phaeton and told him that they didn't believe his father was a god. He was so upset that at last his mother said she would take him to see Phoebus. Perhaps the god could think of some way to prove to the boys at school that Phaeton's father really was the sun god.

'Many weeks later, they arrived at the magnificent eastern palace. Phoebus was overjoyed to see his son and when he heard what the trouble was, he offered the boy his crown. Phaeton was not sure that anyone would believe him just because he had a golden crown.

'"Father," he said, "Would you let me drive your chariot across the sky? If the boys saw me doing that they would have to believe me."

'Both his parents tried to turn him aside from this mad idea. "It takes all my strength to control the horses," said his father. "How do you think you will manage?" But nothing they said could put the boy off. Sadly Phoebus dressed his son in a suit of armour to protect him from the heat and told him what to do.

'"Don't swerve away from the track," he said, "and don't, whatever you do, use the whip or the horses will bolt."

'Phaeton was pleased and proud to be driving his father's chariot across the heavens but the heat bothered him and it was all he could do to hold the team on its course. Time after time he was only just able to keep them on the track. It seemed to be taking ages to get to the highest point. After a more violent swerve than all the others, Phaeton forgot his father's words and flicked at the animals with his whip.

'The horses went crazy, plunging and rearing wildly. The more the boy tried to rein them in, the worse things got. When they soared high above the track, he became dizzy looking down at the vast depths below. When they shot down earthwards, they got so close to the ground that the grass was scorched. Lakes dried up, rivers changed their courses and forests caught fire. The Sahara was turned in an instant from a pleasant area of farmland to the desert we know today.

'Now, totally out of control, the chariot lurched along the paths of heaven. To prevent any more damage Jupiter, the lord of the gods, took a thunderbolt and hurled it at the terrified horses. The missile destroyed the chariot and cut the horses free, but Phaeton,' Cornelius paused and looked at his son, 'Phaeton was killed.'

There was a short silence and then Marcus said in a small voice, 'Sorry Father; I won't do it again.'

8 Maiden Castle

This man's name is Vespasian. He was the commander of the Second Legion, the *Augusta*, as it was called. His legion was sent to Britain to conquer the tribes in the southern part of the country. Suetonius, a Roman writer, tells us that Vespasian's legion captured over twenty fortified towns. One of these towns was Maiden Castle in Dorset.

This is Maiden Castle. Apart from its great ditches it doesn't look much like a stronghold. But here is what it must have looked like in AD 43 or 44 as it faced Vespasian's soldiers. You can see that it is not as big as a modern town. But it does have streets, houses and barns.

Between 1934 and 1937 a team of archaeologists began to dig at Maiden Castle. The team was led by Sir Mortimer Wheeler. From the skeletons and objects the archaeologists found, we know something about the

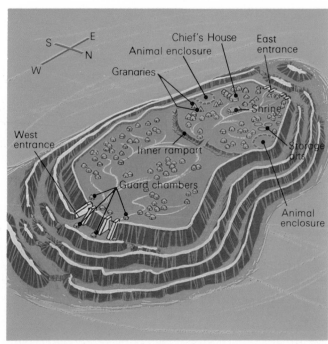

fierce battle Vespasian fought here.

The tribesmen were not afraid of the legions. Their stronghold had always kept them safe from their enemies. From the ditches their warriors could hurl pebbles as big as apples. They used slings to throw them further. Above all, the tribe would be fighting downhill whilst the enemy was struggling up. But the town had never faced a well-drilled Roman army; nor one with siege weapons.

9 The Attack

When the legions arrived they did not begin to fight straight away. Vespasian and his officers rode round the hill several times looking for the weakest place to attack. They decided on the eastern gates.

Next day the chief of the tribe and his men looked down from the gates. They saw the Romans slowly wheeling their siege engines into position. The catapults and ballistas came near enough to hurl rocks and shoot bolts at the Britons. But the Romans were out of range of the British slings.

Soon the bombardment began. It drove the defenders out of the lowest ditch and splintered one of the big wooden gates. Then some of the legionaries formed themselves into a 'testudo' or tortoise. You can see from the picture on page 39 why it was called a tortoise. The men fought their way through the maze of ditches towards the damaged entrance. Those in the middle of the tortoise carried a huge log. They would use it to batter down the broken gate.

While this was going on the Romans were hurling javelins and more stones at the Britons. Every time a defender showed his head above the ramparts he was risking his life. At last the trumpets sounded the advance. The main body of the legionaries put their shields above their heads. Led by their officers they charged towards the town. Soon the Romans were swarming up the slope. They captured ditch after ditch, leaving dead and wounded tribesmen behind them. In the last ditch they came to some huts and quickly set them on fire. As the smoke and flames rose into the sky the legionaries burst through the great gates.

The tribesmen and even their wives fought fiercely but they were no match for the Romans. By the late afternoon the few remaining defenders were forced to give up and the battle was over.

The next day the prisoners had to bury

their dead. There was no time to hold proper burial ceremonies. Food and drink were put in most of the graves to help the dead warriors in the afterlife. The Romans pulled down the massive gates at the west end of the town. Then they destroyed the rest of the defences. Vespasian selected hostages and his army moved off to their next battle.

Here are some of the things that were found by the archaeologists. They are now in the museum at Dorchester. Many of the skulls had been split by Roman swords. One man must have died during the first bombardment of the gate. You can see a catapulta bolt sticking in his spine. This man below is holding a joint of lamb. Somebody must have thought he might get hungry on his way to the next world.

10 The Signifer

This tombstone is from Caerleon on the Welsh border. It tells us about a Roman soldier. The writing means: 'To the Gods of the Underworld. Gaius Valerius Victor, son of Galeria of Lugdunum,* standard bearer to the Second Legion, *Augusta*. He served seventeen years and died aged forty-five.'

A legion had a brass eagle as its main emblem. It was carried by a senior officer and always had a small group of men to guard it. It was a disgrace to lose the eagle in battle. Romans often fought for years to get back one which had been captured from them.

Gaius did not carry the legion's eagle. He was a Signifer, or standard bearer. Every legion had several cohorts, each divided into centuries. Every group had its own standard so there must have been about sixty of them in a legion.

A Signifer had to be brave but not so brave that he led his men into danger when there was no need. Gaius had joined the legion in France, the country where he was born. He trained under strict centurions. Soon he became a good soldier and was promoted.

In the year AD 43, the Emperor Claudius ordered the Augusta and three other legions to attack Britain. The commander of the Augusta was Vespasian. He later became emperor himself.

Vespasian led his men to victory in thirty

A Roman marching camp

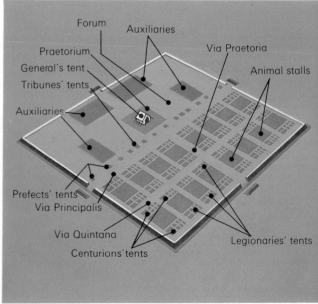

*Lugdunum was the Roman name for Lyon in France.

battles. The legion captured the Isle of Wight and over twenty hill forts. You can read on pages 38 and 39 how they took Maiden Castle.

Every time a legion stopped for the night, the soldiers made a camp. They set up the tents and made a wall of earth all around them. Four years after they landed, the Romans had overrun most of south-east England. Some of the camps were rebuilt in wood, brick and stone. One of these camps became the fortress of Glevum (Gloucester) and another became Isca (Caerleon).

The soldiers made roads to join the forts. The Second Legion made Caerleon its base. Some of the soldiers left it from time to time to do other jobs. Some started a lead mine in Somerset. Some built part of Hadrian's wall.

Gaius, as a sort of senior sergeant, had to look after his men when they were at Isca. He held inspections and helped train the new recruits. He saw that each soldier got his pay and he ran the camp savings bank.

We don't know how or when Gaius died. There are not many records of the period. Tombstones can give us a few facts with which to make a picture of life in those days. For example, this stone, bearing the unlikely name of Longinus Sdapezematygus, tells us that he was a Greek, aged 40, who had served as a horse soldier. Those who dug up the stone in Colchester say that it was probably knocked over and damaged by some of Boudicca's rebels.

11 Roman Ships

We don't know as much about the ships the Romans used as we do about the villas and towns in which they lived. The remains of Roman buildings are often found. Ships are made of wood and wood quickly rots away in the salt sea water. But the Romans did write about their ships. Sometimes they carved pictures of them on buildings and monuments. Here is a picture of the types of ship Vespasian would have used to bring his legionaries and their baggage from Gaul to Britain.

Remains of a Roman ship found at Blackfriars in London

1 1 15 The Baths

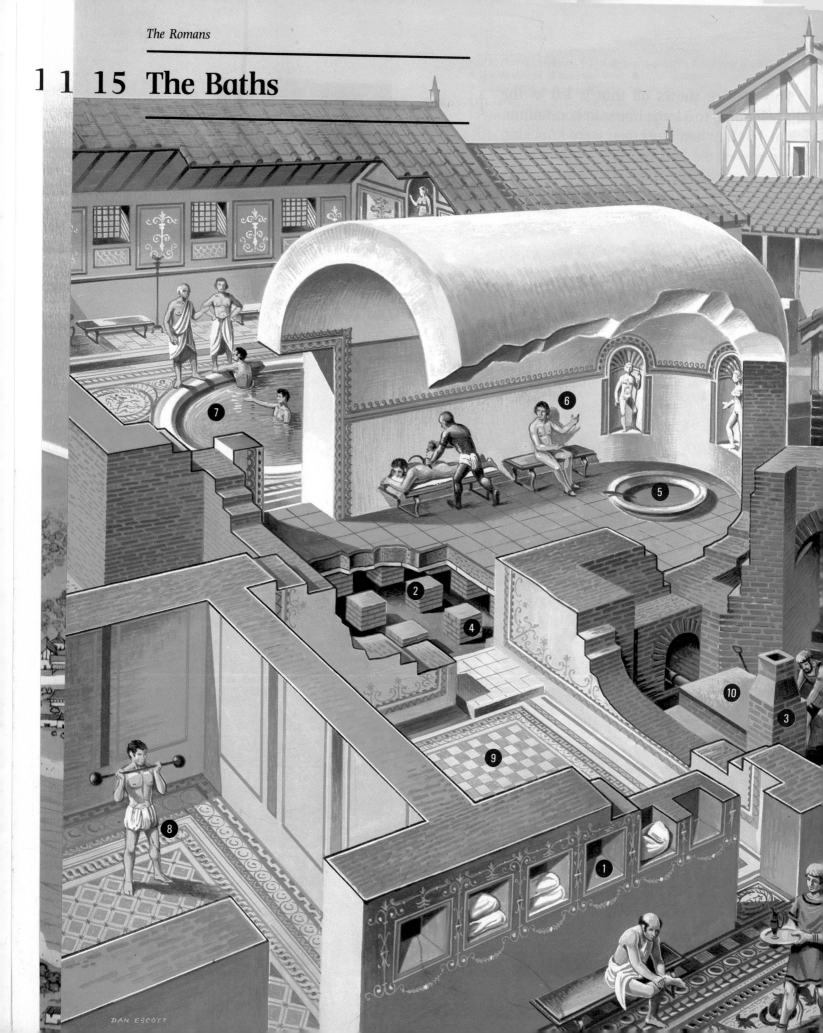

DAN ESCOTT

Some Roman houses had Turkish baths and others had saunas. Very rich families might have had both. A Turkish bath will steam you, the sauna uses dry heat. In both cases the idea is to make you perspire. Let's pretend you are going to have a Turkish bath.

You leave your clothes in the first room (1). In the second one you might do some press-ups or weight-lifting to start you sweating. At a public bath, there would have been a gymnasium where you could join in a ball game. Roman children were fond of playing 'touch' or leapfrog there.

The next room is warmer and the last one hotter still. The Romans kept up the heat by means of a hypocaust (2), which you can see in the picture.

Look at the slaves stoking the furnace (3). The gases from the fire are swirling round the brick pillars (4) and making the tiled floor hot. There is a huge basin of water in the corner (5). If you splash the water on to the tiles, it will cause clouds of steam and make the air misty.

There wasn't any soap in Roman times, so you will probably get a slave to rub you down with olive oil (6). You feel yourself getting hotter. All the little pores in your skin open, and the oil and perspiration carry away the dirt. Then you have to scrape off all the dirty oil with an implement called a strigil.

You walk to the next room and dive into a cold plunge bath (7). You swim a few strokes and climb out, shaking the hair out of your eyes. A good rub down with a rough towel makes you glow all over. All you have to do now is pull your tunic on and slip your feet into your sandals.

Strigil and oil pot

We don't know who the people were who lived in the house at Lower Thames Street, nor do we know how it came to be in ruins. By AD 450 the remains of the bath house seem to have been used as a rubbish dump. By that time, the soldiers had gone home to defend Rome from its enemies. The Saxons invaded most of south-east England.

A Saxon warrior, wandering through the half-empty city, noticed water gushing up through broken bricks. He wondered where it was coming from. He did not know that it was the spring which had fed the baths. He climbed on to the heaps of rubble, searching for the source. Unluckily for him, one of the two brooches which fastened his cloak came undone and dropped down out of sight. He couldn't find it.

The brooch didn't see the light of day again until 1968 when the rest of the Roman building was dug up. Not far from where the Saxon had lost his brooch, the diggers also found a number of Roman coins. The family had most likely hidden them when the Saxons first attacked London. They were no doubt hoping that the invaders would go away and that they would be able to come and live in the house again.

Key to Roman Baths **1** lockers for clothing **2** hypocaust **3** chimney **4** pilae, **5** bowl of cold water **6** caldarium **7** cold plunge bath **8** gymnasium **9** tepidarium

Work Section

Understand your Work

1 Fishbourne
1 What does the word 'derelict' mean?
2 What part does the weather play in making empty houses derelict?
3 Why do we paint woodwork?
4 Which of these materials are more likely to decay, and which will survive for a long time: a) wood; b) cloth; c) stone; d) pottery; e) iron; f) gold?
5 What are tiles?
6 Did the workmen know what they had found?
7 Who had owned the house?
8 How old were the objects?
9 Look at the photograph of the derelict house on page 22. Are there any houses in your own neighbourhood that look like this?
10 The picture on page 23 shows a reconstruction of Fishbourne palace. What is meant by 'reconstruction'?

2 The People
1 Where is Rome? Find it on the map on page 24.
2 Were the Romans always a powerful, warlike people?
3 How did the Romans deal with their enemies?
4 Where was Gaul?
5 Which emperor's armies conquered Britain?
6 What was a legion?
7 Why did the Romans invade Britain?
8 Which part of Britain do you think they invaded first?
9 Describe what you can see in the picture at the top of page 25.
10 Look at the coins in the pictures. What are they made of?

3 The Family
1 How might archaeologists be able to tell that the house was Roman?
2 What is the name of the elder boy?
3 How is the boys' bedroom different from the place where the Celtic children sleep?
4 Why is the lavatory next to the bathroom?
5 What is central heating?
6 What is a Magister? Do you know any similar English words?
7 Where is the school?
8 Do the boys always go to school on the cart?
9 Look at the picture of the villa on page 26. Are there any parts of it that are like your own house? What parts of it are different?
10 Look at the picture of the breakfast table on page 27. What things might you have on your own breakfast table that the Romans couldn't have had?

4 The School
1 Is the Roman classroom like your own?
2 How are your own lessons different from those of the Roman children?
3 What language did the Romans use?
4 How did the children learn to write?
5 Why didn't the children write in exercise books?
6 Why did Roman children find it hard to do sums?
7 School finishes soon after midday. How much longer is your own school day? Remember that Roman children probably started earlier than you.
8 Would you enjoy the sort of food the children had for lunch?
9 Look at the picture on page 28. How are the clothes the children are wearing different from your own?
10 Choose one of the photographs on page 29. Describe the objects in it.

5–6 Making a Living/In the Town
1 What is the family business?
2 Who does the work on the farm?
3 What is a shrine?
4 What is a slave?
5 Do all slaves work on farms?
6 What is a magistrate?
7 What happens at the gymnasium?
8 Where has Gaius Julius Decuminus come from?
9 Describe the shrine in the picture on page 30.
10 Describe the market scene in the picture on page 32.

8 Maiden Castle
1 Who wrote about Vespasian in Britain?
2 How do we know about the battle at Maiden Castle?
3 What was the *Augusta*?
4 What was the main advantage the defenders had?
5 What is a siege?

9 The Attack
1 What was the weakest point in Maiden Castle's defences?
2 Why couldn't the Britons damage the Roman siege weapons?
3 Why was a testudo so called?
4 Why do you think Vespasian took hostages?
5 Why were the Britons buried with food and drink?

10 The Signifer
1 How old was Gaius Valerius Victor when he joined the legion?
2 Aquila is the Latin word for eagle. What do you think an Aquilifer was?
3 Where was Gaius born?

4 What did the soldiers do each night?

5 What is a cohort?

6 Apart from fighting, what other jobs did soldiers do?

7 What did the Romans call Caerleon?

8 What duties did a Signifer have?

9 Look at the picture of Gaius Valerius Victor on page 40. Describe what he is wearing. Why do you think his standard has a sharp point at the end of its pole?

10 Look at the illustration of the marching camp on page 40. Now find the Roman fort in the plan of London on pages 48 and 49. In what ways is the camp like the fort?

12 The Ninth Legion

1 Where is Lindum?

2 How many men were there in the Ninth Legion?

3 What were tribunes and legates?

4 Of which tribe was Boudicca queen?

5 Apart from armour and weapons, what did the soldiers have to carry?

6 What was the name of the Ninth Legion?

7 Where is the body of Gaius Saufeis?

8 What might have happened to the Ninth Legion?

9 Copy or trace the picture of Gaius Saufeis and label the pieces of equipment he is carrying on your picture.

10 Look at the battle scene on page 45. How can you tell the Celts from the Romans?

13 An Unsolved Murder

1 When was Hadrian's wall built?

2 Find Hadrian's wall on a map.

3 Do we know much about life at Housesteads fort?

4 Why were the soldiers kept busy?

5 Where was the civilian settlement at Housesteads?

6 Was the shop where the murder took place inside the fort?

7 What are loaded dice?

8 How do we know that the man was killed with a sword?

14–15 Roman London/The Baths

1 Did all the flats or houses in Roman London have their own bathrooms?

2 What was the Latin name for London?

3 What was a strigil?

4 Did the Romans use soap?

5 Who invaded Britain when the Roman legions left?

6 What is a hypocaust?

7 What methods of heating water do we have that the Romans could not have known about?

8 What two discoveries were made in 1968?

9 Look at the picture of the baths on page 50. What is happening to the man lying on the bench?

10 Does the picture show the places where the bathers would leave their clothes?

Use your Imagination

1 Imagine that all the people in your neighbourhood suddenly leave. Nobody goes near the place for five hundred years. Pretend you are the archaeologist who discovers your house. Report what you find.

2 What is meant by 'once you start conquering, it's hard to stop'?

3 You are one of the Roman children and have just woken up. Describe the room you are in and the things that you can see around you.

4 Marcus's school has only ten pupils. Would you like your own school to be that size? List some good points and bad points about small schools.

5 In what ways do you think a Roman farm was different from the farm of today?

6 You are Vespasian. You have to make a speech to your soldiers explaining how you are going to take the Castle. Warn them how the Celts will fight and explain why you are sure you will win.

7 Why were the standards and the eagle important during a battle?

8 Read about the murder at Housesteads on pages 46 and 47. Which parts of the story can we be sure are true?

9 Imagine you are going to sail on one of the ships shown on pages 42 and 43. Describe how you prepare for the voyage. Then describe the ship itself and how you leave port.

10 Imagine that you were a friend of Gaius Saufeis. Tell us how he fought his last battle and how you helped bury him.

11 Imagine you have just had a bath in a Roman house. Describe what happened to you.

12 Do you think there are still many Roman remains waiting to be discovered in places like London, York and Lincoln? Or have we found everything worth finding by now?

Further Work

1 Find out from your local museum where your nearest Roman sites are. Ordnance Survey publishes a map of Roman Britain. Try and visit some of the sites.

2 Make and eat a Roman meal. You should be able to find Roman recipes in the cookery section of your library.

3 Your group or class could make a collection of Roman stories. The library will be able to help.

4 Draw and label a picture of a first-century Roman soldier. Then make a picture or a model of the attack on Maiden Castle.

5 Find out what happened to Boudicca and the Iceni.

6 Make a plan of a Roman marching fort or a Roman town.

1 Romans and their Gods

This is a scene in a Roman temple in London. It is the temple of Jupiter, the most important of the Roman gods. The visitor prays to Jupiter that he will have a safe journey. He pours a little wine on the altar in front of the statue as an offering.

He could choose to go to any of the temples in Roman London, each built to house the statue of a different god. On the opposite page are some of the gods.

The Romans don't mind how many gods the people worship. Just as long as no one says that his is the only god, he can pray to dozens of different ones on the same day if he wants to. The Romans have even brought back a few gods from abroad. They have built altars and

temples to these gods too. The law says that the citizen must also bow down to statues of the emperor. The emperors of Rome do not like the gods of Britain. This is probably because the Druids refused to let the Celts make peace with the legions. However, Celtic gods are still worshipped in some places, sometimes by Romans themselves.

1–3 Celtic gods; *4* Mercury; *5* Mars; *6* Mithras; *7* Mars
left Part of an altar from the Temple of Jupiter in London

2 The Christians

Christian secret sign from Ephesus

There is another group the Romans cannot stand. These are the Christians who will not bow down to any statue at all. The emperors put them in prison, flog them or throw them to the lions in the arena. Even in Britain the Christians have to keep their beliefs hidden.

They meet where and when they can. For safety's sake, they have to have passwords and secret signs. This is so that a Christian will know if a stranger is a friend or an enemy.

For three hundred years Christians were arrested, tortured and killed. The Romans thought they were trouble-makers but the more they tried to stamp out the followers of Christ, the more of them there were.

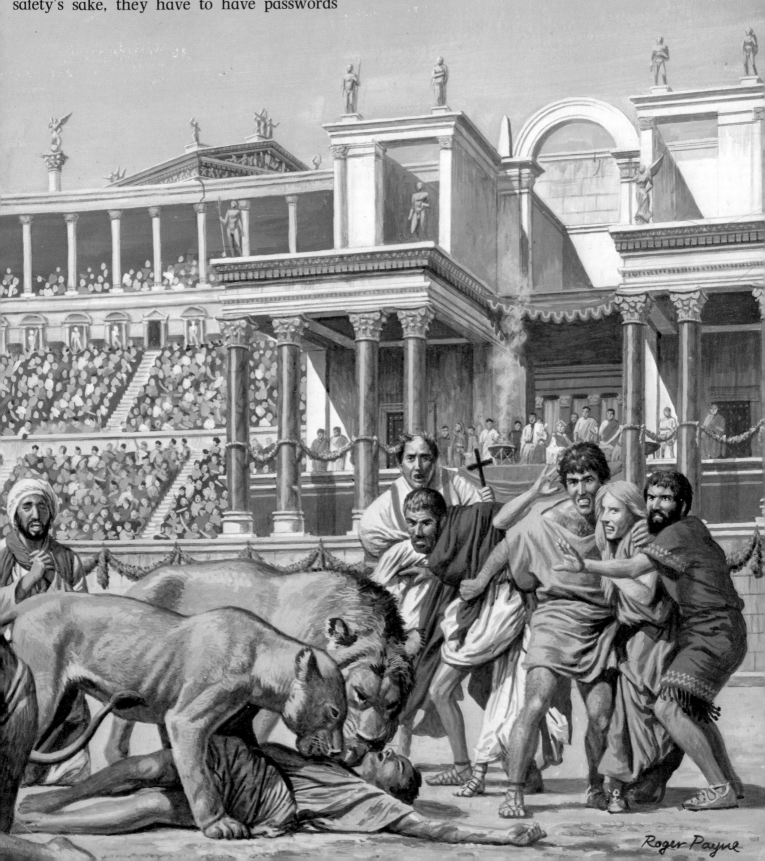

Roger Payne

3 St. Alban

Have you ever been to St. Alban's in Hertfordshire? It was an important town in Roman times and some ancient parts of it can still be seen. If you travel by coach, you will probably get out in the car park and go to look at the finds in the museum. Here are pictures of some of them.

Shell mosaic

Statue of Venus

Lamp chimney

They give you an idea of what life must have been like for the people who lived in Verulamium, as they called it, nearly 2,000 years ago. These museum objects are not all that there is to see. You can go and look at the ruins of a Roman villa with its underfloor heating still in place. You might like to trace the remains of the town walls and gateways and see what is left of the Roman shops and the theatre. If you did all that, you would probably be tired out with walking. You won't have the energy to do more than look at the church in the distance. It's too far away and it isn't Roman anyway.

But why isn't the modern town still called Verulamium? The reason is quite interesting.

When the Romans had been in Britain for over two hundred years, a man named Diocletian became emperor. He found the empire too big to run all by himself, so he split it into two halves, the Eastern and Western Empires. Then he turned to the problem of the Christians.

There were more of them than ever. There were Christians in the army and even in the emperor's own palace. The trouble was that they seemed to be willing to die rather than give up their beliefs. This made many ordinary Romans think that it must be a fine religion if men and women would sooner face death than give it up. So more people became followers of Jesus.

In the year 303, Diocletian gave an order that everything the Christians owned was to

Reconstruction of the forum at St. Albans

A town house

The theatre

be taken from them, their churches torn down and the people themselves made into slaves.

A Christian in Verulamium was warned one night that the soldiers were coming to arrest him. Someone had told the officer that he was not only a Christian but a priest as well. He decided that the best thing he could do was to try to get away from the town as quickly as possible.

Unluckily for him, the soldiers saw him as he was leaving the house and they gave chase. He ran as fast as he could, down streets, across squares and through narrow alleys. He doubled round the side of the theatre and along the back of the silent, empty shops.

He stopped to listen and catch his breath. A door opened near him and a slave girl beckoned him in. She had heard the sounds of people running and had come to see what was happening. She was also a Christian, a slave working for an army officer named Albanus, or Alban. She recognized the priest but before she could hide him, Alban himself appeared.

They had to tell him the truth and he asked why the priest didn't give up his faith and save himself from death. The priest replied and they went on talking for most of the night. Then the soldiers started a house-to-house search. When they came to Alban's house, he had changed clothes with the priest and taken his place. The priest escaped but Alban was put to death.

In later years, Christians were allowed to worship openly and their religion became the official one for the whole empire. The Christians in the town built their new church on the spot where Alban had been executed. The Church in Rome made him a saint. A new town grew up round the local church. It was called St. Albans in his memory. St. Albans is still there but Roman Verulamium lies in ruins.

A modern representation of St. Alban

4 Saxon Raids

At the time that Alban was born, a danger appeared to those who were Christians and those who were not. To find out what it was, let us pretend we can go back into the past and watch what is happening. We are looking at a fishing village in Roman Britain. The year is 285. The village is in ruins. Everything seems to have been smashed, stolen or burnt. Let's ask one of the boys from the village how it happened.

'What's been going on here, Tiso?'

'I'm not sure myself yet. The men were loading their nets on to the boats, ready to go fishing, when I spotted three ships making for the shore. I knew they were not our ships. They weren't Roman ones either. They were long and wide and had neither mast nor sail. The crew were all rowing with long oars. Our

above and right Weapons of the time

men were not sure what to do. They didn't know if the strangers were going to be friendly or not. Most of our men went up to the village to find what weapons they could. Marwed has gone to the fort to fetch the centurion.'

'*What happened next?*'

'Well, the strangers ran their ships on to the beach and started to walk towards us. They were quite tall with fair hair and they were all carrying shields and swords or axes. My father tried to talk to them but they just knocked him down. There was nothing we could do except hide. There were far too many of them.'

'*What did they want?*'

'Anything they could get. They loaded their ships with our corn, sheep and valuables. I think they even took some of the older children. My friend Dracus was carried off. Then they set fire to the village. We're bound to starve'.

As Tiso is talking, a column of legionaries with their centurion is marching down to the beach. They are far too late. The three Saxon ships are black specks on the horizon.

'Saxons, eh?' says the centurion. 'Don't worry, we'll have a working party sent out to help rebuild the village and we'll send some rations over. Next time they dare show their faces, we'll be ready for 'em'.

Unluckily for the Britons, more Saxons came in the next few years. Once in a while the Roman soldiers caught them but most of the time, the raiders attacked so quickly that they were gone before anything could be done.

5 The End of the Empire

Collapse of the Roman empire

Britain was not the only part of the empire to be attacked. Every few years, news would arrive that enemy tribes had broken through the frontiers. The commander of the British legions would then have to take his soldiers to help defend the empire against the hordes of wild tribesmen who wanted to smash it.

When that happened, the Saxon raiders had more time to murder and plunder. They knew that there were no troops about so they moved further inland. They brought more

ships from their homelands in Germany and Denmark. There were plenty of Saxons willing to row hundreds of miles across the North Sea if there were easy pickings to be had at the end of the voyage.

Nearly all of the Britons who had lived in villages on the coast thought it better to move away to where they felt safer. The Saxons followed them up the rivers leading inland. Then they would fill their ships with loot from places ever farther from the sea.

Sometimes the Saxons would come upon a small town. They were not interested in the underfloor heating of the houses, nor in the temples, churches and baths. All they wanted was the treasure inside them. They smashed down doors and stole whatever they fancied. When they had got all they wanted, they often had a feast. A few of the cattle they had taken would be killed, roasted and eaten.

They did not admire the fine villas. They were just as likely to break up tables and stools to make a fire in the middle of a beautiful mosaic floor.

When the legions had dealt with the troubles in the empire, they came back to Britain and drove off the Saxons once more. Many years later, the tribes in Europe broke through the frontiers in several places at once. The Roman troops had to leave yet again.

If you had been down in the docks at Dover on a spring morning in the year 410, you would have seen more soldiers than you had ever seen before. They are being marched on to the ships.

The little girl does not know it but this time the legions will not be coming back. Before her life is over, Rome itself will have been conquered and the empire will be at an end.

6 Saxon Settlements

When the Saxons found that the legions did not come back, they spread further into England. Then they heard that Rome itself had been captured. Now they could stay here for good, provided they could beat the Britons.

One thing was sure. If they stayed, they would have to change their way of life. It was all very well raiding villages and towns but they couldn't keep on doing this. Once they had driven out the Britons, there was nothing left to steal because there was nobody to raise cattle or plant corn.

A few Saxons came as families with wives and children. Others married young British women. The settlers gave their villages Saxon names which often end in 'ing', 'ham' or 'ton'. The only British words they took over were the names of nearby hills and rivers which they may have learned from their British wives.

The Britons called all the invaders 'Saxons' but there were many different tribes, such as Jutes, Angles and even Franks.

What did the Britons do without the legions to help them? We can't be sure but there are legends, or stories, told. One of these says that the Britons found a man to train them and lead them against the Saxons. The legends say his name was Arthur. If he existed,

this is what Arthur might have looked like. Later, all sorts of wild legends were invented with Arthur as their hero. Most of them couldn't have been true.

It is possible that there was a great fighter called Arthur and that he fought many battles against the Saxons. He may have stopped them taking over the whole of England – for a time. The Saxons gave up trying to push westward and seemed content to stay in the lands they had already taken. Then, perhaps a hundred years after Arthur's time, they were on the move again.

This time there was no great leader to stop them. They beat the Britons and drove them into the mountains of the west and north. They set up their own Saxon kingdoms and began farming the land.

Do you remember the Saxon warrior who

The Saxon's brooch

lost one of his cloak brooches while he was wandering over the ruins of a Roman bath house? We don't know his name but we think we know where he went. He belonged to a band of Saxons which set up a kingdom to the south of the River Thames. It was actually named 'The South Kingdom'. In the Saxons' own language it was 'Suth Rige'. It sounded, perhaps, like 'Soo-three-er'. If you don't say it carefully, it ends up as 'Surrey'.

Our Saxon died and was buried at Mitcham in Surrey. Of course, we can't be completely certain that it was the same man but a brooch was buried with him. It was the twin of the one found in London.

Suthrige kingdom

7 Angles or Angels?

When the Saxons first came to Britain, they had gods and goddesses of their own. We know some of these because most of the days of the week are named after them. Tiw, the war god, Woden, the father of the gods and Thor, the god of thunder, gave their names to Tuesday, Wednesday and Thursday. Friday comes from the goddess Frig. The Saxon days of the sun and moon are our Sunday and Monday.

Pope Gregory

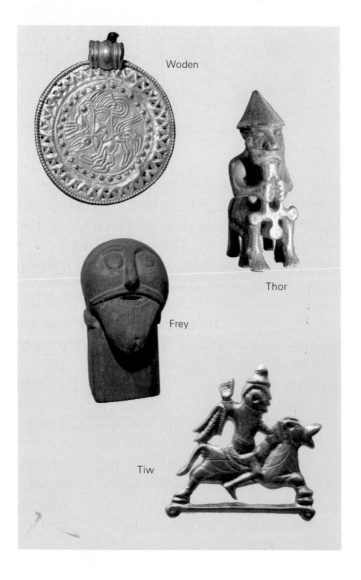

Woden

Thor

Frey

Tiw

Christianity died out in England with the coming of the Saxons. There were of course a few Christians among the Britons who had been driven westward to Wales and Cornwall or northward towards Scotland. In these British lands the knowledge of Jesus was kept alive.

Gregory was the son of a rich Christian family in Rome. He became a judge. Then his father died and left him a fortune. He gave it all away and went to live as a poor monk in a monastery. In a few years, he was put in charge of the monastery as abbot. The Bishop of Rome asked him to help organize the Church which was growing fast.

Rome had once been the capital of a great

empire. Now it was becoming the chief city of the Christians. Sad to say, there was at least one thing that had not changed since the days of the emperors. This was slavery.

One day Gregory was passing the slave market when he saw some boys with fair hair who were about to be sold. Their skins were pale and Gregory was puzzled. Most slaves were dark haired and brown skinned. He asked a man where they came from. 'Angle land,' said the man. 'They are Angles.'

Gregory said, 'They look more like angels than Angles.' The man looked surprised.

'They are nothing like angels,' he said. 'They are fierce, savage heathens.'

'Are they indeed?' said Gregory. Then he added, half to himself, 'How wonderful it would be to go to Angle land and tell them about Jesus Christ.'

He put this idea to the bishop and to his surprise, he was allowed to go. Joyfully, he got ready. There was little to pack. He and the monks he chose to go with him took only a

little food. They would be staying in a different monastery each night and walking all day.

They had travelled for only three days when they were overtaken by a messenger on horseback. He told them that the bishop was dead and that they must return to Rome. Gregory found that the old man had died of the plague. Christians were beginning to look up to the bishop as head of the whole Church, or Pope, which actually means 'Father'.

Gregory realized that everyone wanted him as the next leader. He tried to say he was not good enough to be Pope but there was no one else to take on the job. He was so busy in his new position, he knew he would never go to the land of his 'angels'. He didn't forget them, though.

In the year 596 he sent for Augustine, a monk from his old monastery. Augustine was told that he had been chosen to lead a team of monks to rescue the Angles from their heathen ways.

8 The Missionaries

left St. Augustine from a medieval manuscript

Early in the spring of the year 597 Augustine left Rome for Angle land with forty monks. The first part of their journey followed the footsteps of Gregory, but soon they had passed the place where he had turned back. They pressed on, talking excitedly of what they would do when they got to Angle land.

They met a cloth merchant leading a train of horses with packs on their backs. He asked them where they were going. He seemed surprised when they told him, 'Angle land'.

'I wouldn't go to England if you paid me a fortune,' he said. The monks wanted to know what he meant. He told them that the English were cruel, bloodthirsty savages who hated strangers. 'They won't let you land,' said the merchant, 'or, if they do, you won't get a chance to tell them about Jesus. They will kill you, most likely.'

The monks were frightened and refused to go on. After an argument, they went back to Rome where Gregory tried to calm their fears. 'Of course they are savages,' he said. 'That is why they need the word of God. They will let you land and they will listen to you. Go and do God's work.'

The little band set out again, not very willingly, and after a long journey they landed in east Kent. Augustine held a short service to thank God for their safe arrival and to ask His help in the task before them. It seemed to him that their prayers had been answered when a message arrived from Ethelbert, the King of Kent.

The king ordered Augustine to come and see him. To Augustine's delight, he found that King Ethelbert's wife, Berta, was already a Christian. She persuaded her husband to let the missionaries preach and even to build churches. The first church the monks put up was near the place where they had landed. Its foundations can still be seen amid the ruins of the Roman fort at Richborough. The second tiny chapel was built in Canterbury, the king's chief town. There is a church there to this day. It is called Canterbury Cathedral. Of course, the cathedral wasn't started until long after.

Queen Berta's daughter, Ethelburga, went to the north of England to marry Edwin, King of Northumbria. With her she took Paulinus, one of Augustine's monks. Paulinus did his best to talk Edwin into becoming a Christian but the king was not sure.

One night, after supper in the king's great wooden hall, the talk turned to religion. Edwin asked his thanes, or lords, what they thought. Some were for Paulinus, some were for the old gods. In the silence that followed a bird flew into the hall. It was lit for a moment by the candles and the bright firelight and then it was gone.

Remains of St. Augustine's Church in the Roman fort at Richborough

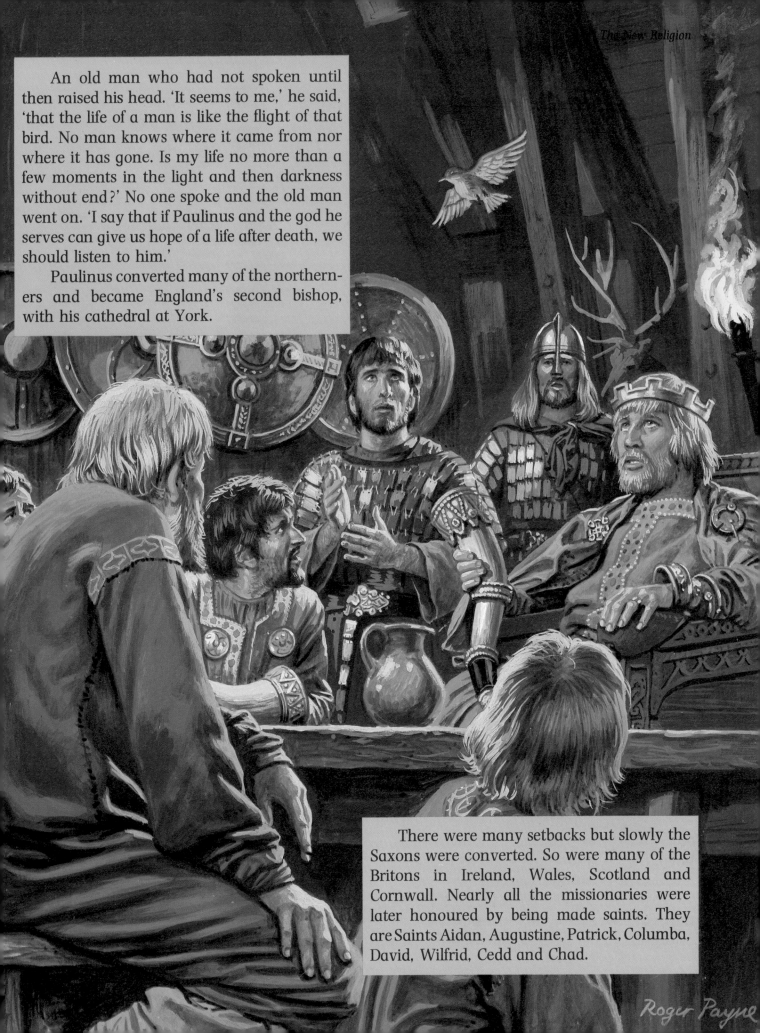

An old man who had not spoken until then raised his head. 'It seems to me,' he said, 'that the life of a man is like the flight of that bird. No man knows where it came from nor where it has gone. Is my life no more than a few moments in the light and then darkness without end?' No one spoke and the old man went on. 'I say that if Paulinus and the god he serves can give us hope of a life after death, we should listen to him.'

Paulinus converted many of the northerners and became England's second bishop, with his cathedral at York.

There were many setbacks but slowly the Saxons were converted. So were many of the Britons in Ireland, Wales, Scotland and Cornwall. Nearly all the missionaries were later honoured by being made saints. They are Saints Aidan, Augustine, Patrick, Columba, David, Wilfrid, Cedd and Chad.

Roger Payne

9 A Ship Burial

The children in this picture are dressed as Vikings. They look as though they are burning a longship. They aren't Vikings and the boat is only a model. The men are celebrating the end of winter at Lerwick in the Shetlands. They call what they are doing 'Up-Helly-Aa' and the reason for the Viking dress is that the Shetland Islands to the north of Scotland once belonged to both Norway and Denmark.

The flaming ship may remind you of the old Norse custom of putting a chief's dead body on his ship, setting fire to it and sending it out to sea. Another kind of ship burial came to light in 1938 when a Suffolk lady named Mrs. Pretty decided to have a closer look at some strangely shaped mounds on her land. She lived close to the River Deben at a place called Sutton Hoo, near Ipswich. The man in charge of the digging was a Mr. Basil Brown.

The diggers cut their way into three of the little hillocks and found that they all contained burials. One was very interesting as the body had been put in a boat before being covered with earth. Unluckily, all three graves had been robbed and there was little to show for the work done.

The following year Mrs. Pretty made up her mind to dig into a new mound, the highest one on her land. No sooner had the digging started, when rows of iron rivets came to light. It was plainly another ship, and a big one at that. Like the other vessel, it showed signs of having been attacked by grave robbers, so Mr. Brown wasn't too hopeful.

However, he went to work, carefully removing the sand from the inside of the ship. Almost all the wood had rotted away and the

only way he could tell where it had been was the pattern of iron rivets. The diggers had just enough time to take out the things they found in the bottom of the hole before the Second World War broke out and the dig had to be filled in again to protect it from enemy bombers.

The objects found in the ship were cleaned and are now preserved at the British Museum. They proved that the ship burial at Sutton Hoo was the richest and most important Saxon archaeological find ever made in Britain.

Belt buckle

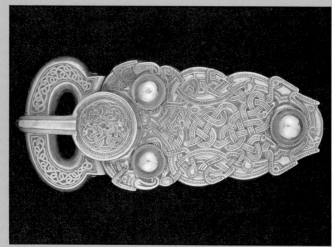

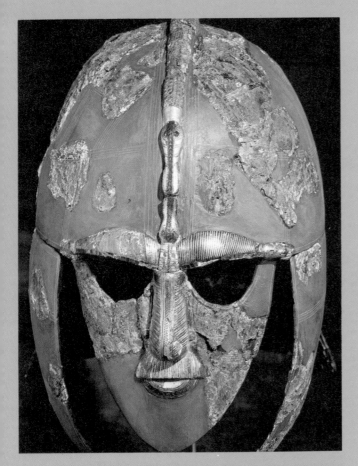

Objects found in the Sutton Hoo ship burial

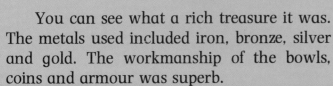

You can see what a rich treasure it was. The metals used included iron, bronze, silver and gold. The workmanship of the bowls, coins and armour was superb.

The value of these things was so great, the experts believe they must have marked the grave of a king. They even think they know which king it was. The coins gave a date in the early 7th century, so it is quite likely that the ruler was Raedwald, Saxon King of East Anglia, who died about 624.

Most of the grave goods show the burial to be that of a pagan chieftain. Most, but not all. There are two silver spoons with Christian markings. Could it be that Raedwald was trying to make sure he went to heaven but was uncertain whether this would be the Christian paradise or the Valhalla of the old Norse gods?

Work Section

Understand your Work

1–2 The Romans and their Gods/Christians

1 Was the temple of Jupiter the only temple in London?
2 Who was Jupiter?
3 Did the Romans worship more than one god?
4 Why didn't the Romans like the Druids?
5 Did the Romans forbid the worship of Celtic gods?
6 Why did the Roman authorities dislike Christianity?
7 What is a password?
8 Did the Romans manage to stamp out Christianity?
9 Look at the red and white stick next to the stone altar on page 55. What do you think it's for?
10 Look at the picture on pages 56 and 57. Describe the scene. Who is sitting under the canopy watching the show?

3 St. Alban

1 What is the Roman name for St. Albans?
2 Why did Diocletian split the empire into two?
3 What happened in AD 303?
4 Why did the Christian priest try to run away?
5 Why did the servant girl help the priest?
6 For whom did she work?
7 Why do you think that Albanus changed places with the priest?
8 What did the Christians build in Verulamium when they were no longer persecuted?
9 Look at the reconstruction of Verulamium on page 58. How is it different from the city centres you know?
10 Look at the picture of the ruins of the theatre on page 59. How do you think archaeologists are able to tell that it *was* once a theatre?

4 Saxon Raids

1 When did the Saxons first begin to raid Britain?
2 How did the villagers make their living?
3 How many Saxon ships took part in the raid?
4 Describe the Saxon ship.
5 How did the Saxons get ashore?
6 Describe a Saxon warrior.
7 What did the Saxons come to steal?
8 Who was supposed to protect the village from attack?
9 Why do you think there are differences in the armour and uniforms of the soldiers shown on pages 40, 41, 44, 45 and 62?
10 Do you think the weapons at the top of page 61 are Roman or not?

5 The End of the Empire

1 Was Britain the only part of the Roman empire to be attacked?
2 Why did the legions have to keep leaving Britain?

3 What did the Saxon raiders do while the Roman soldiers were away?
4 What happened to the Britons who lived on the coast?
5 What were the Saxon raiders looking for?
6 Why didn't the Saxons care about the fine Roman buildings?
7 Where is Dover? Find it on a map.
8 Why did the legions leave Britain for good?
9 Find a lighthouse in the picture on pages 62 and 63.
10 Describe the ships in the picture on pages 62 and 63.

6 Saxon Settlements

1 What did the Saxons do when they realized the legions would not come back?
2 Why couldn't the Saxons continue to raid and steal?
3 There were other invaders besides the Saxons. Who were they?
4 What is a legend?
5 Who was the legendary leader of the Britons?
6 What did the Saxons do when they had their own kingdoms?
7 Where did the Saxon warrior lose his cloak brooch?
8 What Saxon place name has changed to Surrey?
9 Look at the picture of Arthur on page 64. Is it different from other pictures of him you have seen? How?
10 Why do you think the ruler is included in the photograph of the brooches on page 65?

7 Angles or Angels?

1 Which days of the week are named after Saxon gods or goddesses?
2 Who was the god of thunder?
3 In which parts of Britain were there still Christians after the Saxon invasion?
4 Where was Gregory's home?
5 What did Gregory do with his fortune?
6 Where did the slave boys come from?
7 Who gave Gregory permission to go to Angle land?
8 Gregory never finished his journey. What happened to stop him?
9 What things would you expect to be able to buy in a Roman market?

8 The Missionaries

1 In which year did Augustine leave Rome?
2 How many monks did he take with him to England?
3 Why were the monks frightened of the English?
4 Whereabouts in England did Augustine land?
5 Which king sent for him?

6 Which of the monks went to Northumbria?

7 Of what did the flight of a bird remind the old man?

8 What exactly is a missionary?

9 Look at the picture of St. Augustine on page 68. What is the stone object shown in the picture?

10 Make a simple plan of the fort at Richborough. The photograph on page 68 will help you.

9 A Ship Burial

1 Which river runs near Sutton Hoo?

2 Who owned the land where the treasure was found?

3 Who dug out the remains?

4 How did he know that a ship had been buried there?

5 Why had the hole to be filled in again?

6 Where were the treasures cleaned and displayed?

7 Which metals had been used for some of the objects?

8 Which king was probably buried at Sutton Hoo?

9 Look at the picture of the horns on page 71. What do you think they were used for?

10 Use the patterns on the brooch shown on page 70 to make your own picture.

Use your Imagination

1 Why are there no longer temples to many different gods in this country?

2 Imagine the meeting between Albanus, the Christian priest and the slave girl. Write down some of the things they may have said to each other.

3 Imagine that you are Tiso or Dracus. Describe the raid on your village and what will happen now that it is destroyed.

4 Why couldn't the legionaries defend the villagers against the Saxons?

5 A Saxon poet described the ruined forts and towns the Romans left behind as 'the work of giants'. Why did he say this and what do you think he meant by it?

6 Read pages 48 to 51. Then read pages 60 to 65. Now imagine you are the Saxon who lost his cloak brooch. Tell the story of how you find the Roman baths and say what you think of Roman London.

7 Why do you think that Gregory cared about a country he had never visited?

8 What do you think it would be like to be a slave in a strange country?

9 Imagine you are the cloth merchant who met Augustine and his monks. Write a letter to your wife describing the meeting.

10 What do you think of the reasons the old man gave for listening to Paulinus's teachings?

11 Why do you think the Second World War interrupted the excavations at Sutton Hoo?

12 Why do *you* think Raedwald might have had both Christian and pagan objects at his burial?

Further Work

1 Make up a secret sign for yourself and your friends. Why is it hard to discover what other people's signs are?

2 Did religious persecutions stop when the Roman empire became Christian? Can you think of any other times when people have been persecuted for their beliefs?

3 Find out how far it is from Dover to Rome. How long do you think it took the legions to get from Dover to Rome?

4 If you had been in charge of getting the legions away from Dover, you would have had a lot to do. What sort of things would you have had to plan? Think about the number of ships you would need, food supplies, and contacting and assembling the men of the legion. Make a list of the things you would have to do. The picture on pages 62 and 63 may help you.

5 You are the little girl in the picture on pages 62 and 63, or her brother. Tell the story of the parting.

6 Find out all you can about King Arthur. Why do you think we know so little about him?

7 Choose one of the missionaries mentioned in this chapter and find out all you can about him. Write about his life and work.

8 Find out all you can about the Sutton Hoo burial. You might be lucky enough to visit the British Museum and see the objects that were found. Draw some of the objects to illustrate your work.

Chapter Four   The Saxons

1 The Family

Wulfstan is a thane, or lord. He is going to tell us why his people came to England and a little about his family.

'They came in great ships,' he says, 'from the other side of the North Sea, where our home once was. The land there was poor and would not grow very much. We were hungry a lot of the time. We got better at building ships and taking them to sea. If we couldn't grow enough food on our farms we could at least catch fish to eat. It isn't easy to catch fish and it's a lot more dangerous than growing oats.

'After a while, we decided to try to find a better land to settle in. That was years ago, of course, soon after the Romans left Britain. I was born here and so were my three children.

'Cedfric is my eldest child, and Athelm my youngest. Edbur, the only girl, comes in between. Their ages are twelve, nine and seven. Cedfric is already learning to be a thane like me. He is being taught how to use sword and spear so that he can take my place one day.

'As one of the king's chief soldiers, I have to fight for him when there's a war. In peace time I try to protect the villages in this area. I help the farmers by hunting down the wild animals which would eat or damage their crops. All these things Cedfric will have to do when he grows up.

'My other two children are different from Cedfric. Edbur is practical and Athelm is a dreamer but both are clever. No one could say that about Cedfric!

'Edbur is good at embroidery and sewing and she mustn't waste her life married to some farmer. Athelm will never earn his living by farming or fighting. He does nothing very much except stare and wonder. I shall soon have to tell Athelm what I have planned for him. The boy doesn't know it yet but the king has offered him a place in his new school at Winchester.

'Our king, Alfred, thinks that some of the brighter children ought to know how to read and write. I wasn't educated myself; nor was anyone else in this village. I'm not sure whether it's a good thing or not. Look at Eswy, the swineherd's son. Far from reading, he wouldn't even know what a book was. Yet he seems happy enough to look after the pigs and help his father on the farm.

'Now I think of it, none of the children here seem unhappy. Would they be better off if they could speak Latin? All the same, I can't see Athelm ploughing a field. These things may be fine for most of the other children but I suppose he will be better off at school. I'll tell him tomorrow when the king and the bishop come to see how we're getting on with the building of the new church.'

2 A Saxon Village

After the Saxon raiders had driven the Britons away into the hills, or even captured some of them, they set about making their own villages. Often they chose places fairly near river banks.

Much hard work was needed. Trees were chopped down and their roots pulled out by men using teams of oxen. The branches were lopped off the tree trunks. The wood was used to build the first houses.

When the land was cleared, the men shared it out. There were two or three very large fields for crops such as wheat, barley, oats, peas and beans. Most of the animals were kept together in another field where they could eat fresh grass. The men saved some of the grass from part of the field. They dried it and fed it to the animals in the winter. On the edges of the forest, pigs ate acorns and roots.

There were pits for the digging of stone, chalk and clay. Some of the women had beehives for honey. Near the small houses a few vegetables were grown. The women cut reeds from the river's edge. They were for thatching the roofs of the houses and barns. There were very few stone buildings in Saxon England. The thane's house was the biggest in the village but it was made of timber like all the others.

The small huts of the poorer peasants were crowded in the winter. Some farm animals had to be brought inside during the worst of the weather.

The farmers ploughed their long, thin strips of land with oxen. The soil was then raked with a harrow to break up the lumps. When it was fine enough, the seeds were scattered by hand and covered with soil. In the late summer the crops were harvested. It was hard, tiring work.

While the men worked in the fields, the women were busy too. They had to look after the young children and get the meals ready. Peasant women fed chickens, kept bees, milked goats, made cheese and brewed beer from barley. All women, whether rich or poor, had to be able to sew and spin, to weave cloth and make clothes. The poorer wives spent most of their time doing these things. The richer ones had slaves to do much of the work.

3 Saxon Churches

You can see how far the building of the church has got.

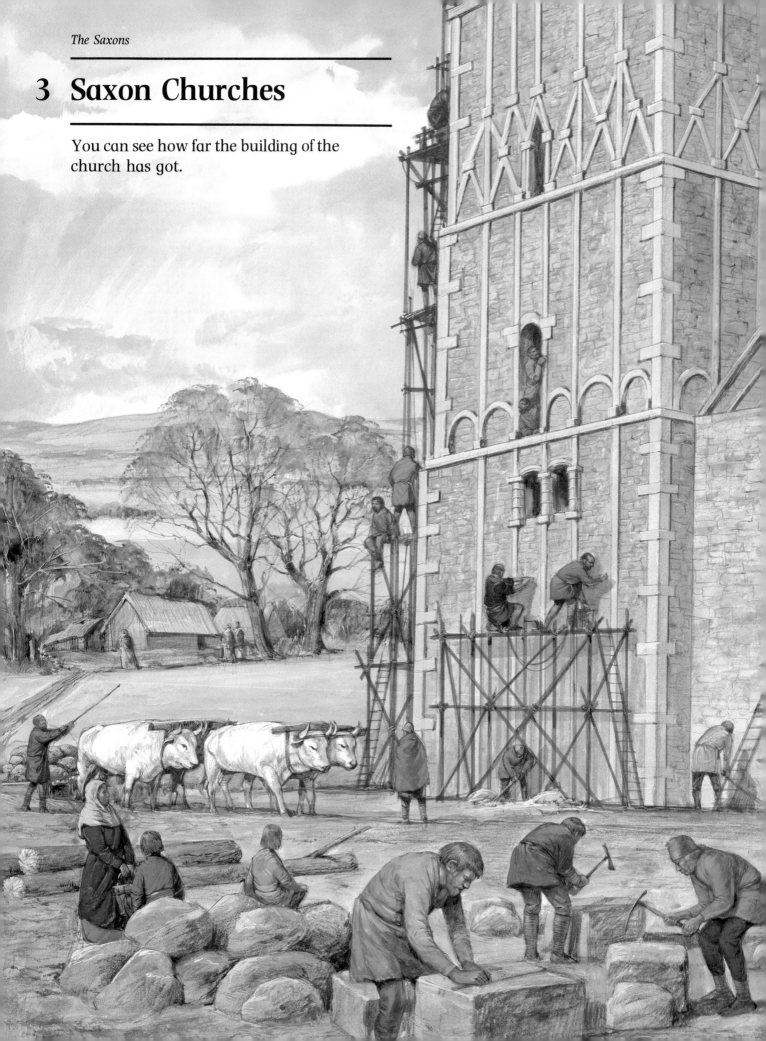

4 King Alfred

When the church is nearly finished, the bishop arrives with a lot of important-looking people. He goes to the stone cross to say prayers for the people of the village. They all kneel down while he is speaking. Athelm keeps staring at the bishop and those who have come with him. Most of them are splendidly dressed. Athelm doesn't know that one of the strangers is King Alfred himself.

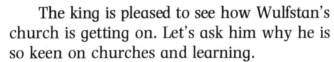

The king is pleased to see how Wulfstan's church is getting on. Let's ask him why he is so keen on churches and learning.

'Well,' he says, 'I was taught to read and write when I was a child and later I learned Latin. I love books and I don't think we'd be any better than the Danes* without them. Nor can we be proper Christians unless some of us can read and learn how we are supposed to behave.

'You know that the Danes have taken half of this land? Well, I got to know them early in my life and I tell you that the way of learning is better than that of barbarism.'

We ask him about the Danes. 'My father was Ethelwulf, King of Essex, Kent and Wessex. When I was about twenty, the Danes attacked our neighbours, the Mercians. My elder brother and I took our soldiers to help them hit back. We won that time but in the next six years a lot happened. The Danes turned on us and when my father and brothers were all killed, I became king.

'We had beaten the Danes and they left us alone for a while. We used the breathing space to build up a fleet of fast, strong ships and

*'Danes' was Alfred's word for the Vikings.

A Saxon church today

strengthen the towns, or 'burghs', as we call them. It was just as well we did, for in the seventh year of my reign, the Danes came back.

'I was driven westward with only a few followers and had to hide for months among the islands of the Somerset marshes. I managed to raise a new army and we beat the Danes so soundly that it was years before they returned to the fight. When they did, we won again.

'Finally, their leader, Guthrum, agreed to sign a treaty with me at a village called Wedmore. I told him he must become a Christian and then promise not to attack us any more. In return, we Saxons let them keep the eastern part of England, or Danelaw, as they called it. They haven't bothered us since!

'We can now turn our minds to thoughts of peace. I want to make our laws fairer and simpler so that everyone knows where he stands. My school at Winchester is a beginning but I'd like to see more of them.

'That reminds me: where's your son Athelm, Wulfstan?'

Athelm is brought before Alfred and Wulfstan tells him he is to be sent to the king's school at the royal town of Winchester. He is too excited to thank the king properly, but the boy's smile shows how pleased he is.

5 Alfred's School

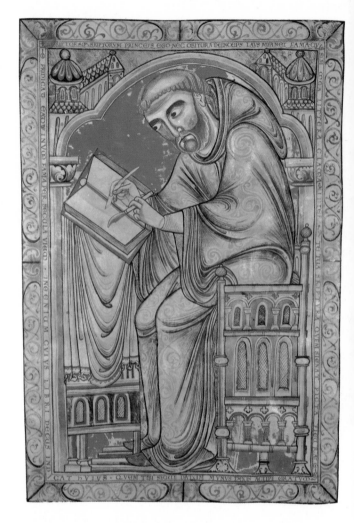

In the years after the Saxons had first become Christian, there were many churches and monasteries built. They needed prayer books and Bibles. The new schools also wanted books. In the days before printing had been invented, every single volume had to be copied out by hand. The Saxons were very good at doing this and soon monasteries in Europe were sending to England for their books. The Saxons had started out as pirates, become farmers and then found themselves the best copiers and artists in the whole of the Christian world.

The monks wrote the words out carefully in ink on parchment. To make the page more beautiful, they painted a coloured design or picture around the first letter of a chapter. Some Saxons did more than copy. They wrote their own books or translated Latin ones into English. A monk named Bede, who lived at Jarrow on the River Tyne, wrote a history of England in Latin. King Alfred himself learned Latin when he was nearly forty so that he could translate works by Latin authors for his people.

During the time of the Danish raids, the Saxons were too busy fighting to worry about books. Now that Alfred had made the Danes agree not to attack his lands, he could think about church matters and teaching the children once more. Let's visit Alfred's new school in his court at Winchester.

It is very early in the morning. The sun is not yet up. A monk goes round the dormitory waking the boys. They wash their hands and faces in cold water and get dressed. There are eleven boys, the youngest only five years old. Two of them are relations of King Alfred. The others, like Athelm, are boys who might make good priests or monks.

The priest blesses the children in Latin and they go off for their first lesson. Their classroom is a monk's cell. It is rather cramped and bare. The teacher sits on the only stool and the children on the floor. The first hour is spent on plain reading and writing in the Saxon language. The second hour is for Latin. They learn Latin prayers by heart but Alfred wants them to be able to understand the language. Then they can write to scholars abroad, no matter where the scholars live, and no matter what language they were brought up to. All educated men know Latin.

After two hours of lessons it is time for breakfast. The children go to a dining room with trestle tables and wooden benches. There is rye bread with goat's cheese, followed by a

bowl of porridge. To wash it down, there are cups of water. Then they must go to their third lesson.

Alfred wants them to be taught about the stars and planets. Those who will be priests when they grow up will then be able to work out the right times for holding the important feasts and fasts of the church year.

After dinner, the children go to another reading and writing lesson. Once the Saxons used letters called runes. By Alfred's time, everyone who can write at all uses the Roman alphabet, both for Latin and Saxon. The children start copying words and sentences on to a writing tablet, rather like the ones Roman schoolboys used.

Other lessons follow as the day goes on. The children are taught about the music used in church and spend a lot of their time studying the Bible itself. So many books are needed that the monastery has its own library. New books and copies of old ones are made in the scriptorium, or writing room.

Pages from two Saxon manuscripts

When the children can write really well, they may be allowed to use quill pens, ink and sheepskin parchment, as the monks do. The copies which the monks make are sent to churches all over Alfred's kingdom and even abroad.

At the end of the children's day, there is a light meal and another service in the chapel. Then, quite early in the evening, they go to bed.

7 A Story

This is Wayland's Smithy near Ashbury in Berkshire. Today we know that it is really a burial chamber from the New Stone Age. The same area has many such reminders of our prehistoric past. Centuries ago, local people made up stories to explain things they didn't understand. This is the story they told about Wayland the Smith.

Some said he was a god. He was a brave warrior, a good hunter and a fine smith. Everyone wanted the beautiful things he made out of iron, silver and gold.

One day he fell in love with a girl and married her. He didn't know that she was really a goddess. After a few years, she grew tired of pretending to be human. When Wayland came home, she was gone.

Thinking she would come back, he made a fine gold ring to give her when she returned. The next day he made another ring, for she was still missing. The weeks turned to months and each day he fashioned a gold ring. He hung them all on a string in the smithy.

News of this strange smith reached the ears of King Nidud, a cruel and greedy man. He sent some of his soldiers to find out if the stories were true.

When the soldiers got to the smithy, Wayland was out hunting. They saw the rings and counted them. 'Seven hundred!' cried one man. 'The smith will never miss one.' When they gave the ring to Nidud, he ordered them to go back and fetch the smith himself. 'If he struggles,' he added, 'tie him up and carry him here.'

Bound hand and foot, Wayland was brought before the king. 'Did you make this?' asked Nidud, holding up the ring. Wayland called him a robber and asked for the ring back. 'Wayland,' said the king, 'we shall have all your rings and anything else you can make.' The furious smith shouted that he would make nothing for a thief.

The king grew angry and gave orders that Wayland's legs should be broken. The king's two sons laughed when this was done. Wayland was kept prisoner in a smithy on an island in the middle of a lake. When his legs had healed, Wayland could scarcely walk. The king told him he would get no more food until he began to make jewellery again. Wayland had to do as he was told or he would have starved but in his heart he planned his revenge.

Secretly he stole small pieces of the metals the king gave him to work with and began to make a pair of wings. If he couldn't escape on foot he would learn to fly.

One night the king's two sons rowed over to the island. They were as cruel and greedy as Nidud himself. They wanted Wayland to hand over some of their father's gold which had been given to the smith for him to use. Wayland asked them if anyone knew they had come. Naturally, they had told no one. Wayland then said that the gold was in a large chest in the corner. As they bent over to lift the lid, he killed them both with an axe.

He cut off their heads, buried the bodies and burned their boat. Using all his skill, he

turned the skulls into silver bowls. Nidud thought the boys were away hunting and suspected nothing. He even admired the new bowls which Wayland had made.

Then Nidud's daughter also paid Wayland's smithy a secret visit but for a very different reason. She told him that she was ashamed of what her father had done. Wayland knew that his vengeance was almost complete when she went on to say that she now hated her parents.

She said that she had fallen in love with Wayland and wanted to go with him. They could use her boat, she suggested. Wayland was sorry for her but had to say that he was already married. She watched in amazement as he strapped on his wings and flew to Nidud's castle.

The king was furious when Wayland told him that his sons were dead and that his daughter hated him. Nidud's archers tried to shoot Wayland as he flew away but they missed. Ever since, he has searched the whole world, looking for his beloved wife.

Work Section

Understand your Work

1 The Family
1 What rank does Wulfstan hold?
2 Why did Wulfstan's people come to England, according to him?
3 What are the names of Wulfstan's children?
4 Which one is the girl?
5 What does Wulfstan do for the king and for his village?
6 What is the king's name?
7 What does Eswy do?
8 What does the king think the cleverest children should do?
9 Describe the clothes Wulfstan and his wife are wearing.
10 Do you think that Cedfric looks as if he enjoys weapon training?

2 A Saxon Village
1 In what sorts of places did the early Saxon settlers build their villages?
2 How did they pull out tree roots?
3 What did they do with the wood from the trees they cut down?
4 What crops did they grow?
5 What did the farm animals eat in the winter?
6 What were the house roofs thatched with?
7 What shape are the strips they plough?
8 What sorts of women have to know how to weave, spin and sew?
9 Compare the Saxon house with the Roman villa on page 26. How are they different?
10 Look carefully at the picture on pages 76 and 77. Find the church, the thane's house, men threshing grain, timber felling, thatchers at work, men ploughing, pig pens, grain stores, and beehives.

3–4 Saxon Churches/King Alfred
1 Where does the bishop say prayers for the villagers?
2 When did King Alfred learn to read and write?
3 Which foreign language was he taught?
4 What was Alfred's word for the Vikings?
5 Who was Alfred's father?
6 How old was Alfred when the Danes attacked Mercia?
7 What is a 'burgh'?
8 Where did Alfred sign a treaty with Guthrum?
9 Look at the picture on pages 78 and 79. Which building methods are still in use today and which have changed?
10 What is the object in front of the church on page 80?

5 Alfred's School
1 How were books produced in the days before printing?
2 Where were books needed?
3 What did the monks write on?
4 How did they make each page more beautiful?
5 What does 'translated' mean?
6 Who wrote a history of England in Latin?
7 Where was Alfred's school?
8 Why did Alfred want the pupils to learn Latin?
9 How is the scene in Alfred's school on page 83 different from your own?
10 How are the books on pages 82 and 83 different from books today?

6 Law and Order
1 How often did a village hold its court?
2 Where did the court meet when the weather was good?
3 Where were very serious cases heard?
4 What were the punishments for serious offences?
5 What is a blood feud?
6 What was wer-gild?
7 What was a trial by ordeal?
8 Why doesn't Wulfstan know what policemen are?
9 Describe what is happening to Hod in the picture on page 85.
10 Which king is shown on the coins on page 84?

Use your Imagination

1 Imagine you are a Saxon helping to make a settlement near a river or in a forest clearing. Describe what has to be done.

2 Why do you think there were no shops in Saxon villages?

3 Imagine you are present at the scene shown in the picture on pages 78 and 79. Describe what is happening and what the new church is like.

4 What sort of things are you taught at school that Saxon children could not have known about?

5 Make an illumination of the first letter of your name. It will help if you look at some of the work of Saxon monks first.

6 Do you think that people in Saxon times did as much travelling as people do today? Give evidence and reasons for your answer.

7 Why do you think that Latin continued to be the most important language even after the Romans had left England?

8 Why do we no longer have trials by ordeal?

9 The tithing system worked quite well in a Saxon village. Why wouldn't it work today?

10 What parts of the Wayland story could be true? Which parts could not possibly be true?

11 Who do you think went to school in Saxon times? Who did not? Why didn't everybody have the same sort of education?

12 Imagine you are one of the children described on pages 74 and 75. Say what your life will be like when you grow up. Say how it will be different from life in our own times.

Further Work

1 Find some examples of Saxon writing of poetry in a modern translation. Choose something you like and put it into your own words. You will be able to get help at your library with this work.

2 Imagine you are the Saxon poet who thought that the Roman ruins were 'the work of giants'. Remember that you will have seen no building larger than a hut before. Find some pictures of Roman ruins and write about them.

3 Now imagine you are the Saxon poet and you have been transported in a time machine to our own time. Write about what you see and feel.

4 Describe and draw some of the Saxon objects in your nearest museum.

5 Early historians often wrote about things that happened in their own times. Sometimes two historians tell the same story. Often two versions of the same story are very different. Why do you think this is?

6 Now try this experiment. Divide the class into five groups. Your teacher tells each group a story about something that happened when she or he was your age. Group 1 hears the story on Monday, group 2 on Tuesday and so on. After the story you can ask your teacher questions. During the following week each member of the group writes his version of the story and the group chooses the one it thinks is the most accurate. Then the teacher reads out the chosen story from each group. Are the stories exactly the same, nearly the same, different or very different?

7 Many towns or cities have names which end in 'ing', 'ham' or 'ton'. This means that they probably started as Saxon settlements. List all the ones you know. You might like to mark them on a map.

8 Here are some Saxon words. Can you guess what they mean? The English equivalents are listed below.

candol nacod æppel spearwa fæder bearn hearpe sprecan furh-wudu biscop lytel screawa gewriten

written apple baby candle sparrow bishop speak small shrew pinetree harp father naked

Chapter Five   The Vikings

1 Viking Ships

It is a misty autumn day in 1955. A fishing boat is just coming into port. The port is Roskilde in Denmark. The engine is puttering happily. As the skipper takes the ship through the narrow channel leading to the harbour, another boat begins to overtake him.

The skipper looks at it angrily. 'The fool,' he mutters, 'there isn't room for two vessels here.' He has to move over and as he does, he feels and hears the bottom of the ship scrape on something under the water. He is lucky that they don't go aground.

When the ship is safely in port, he complains to the harbour master. 'Someone ought to do something about it,' he says. Two years later someone does.

In the summer of 1957, a team of divers went down to see what the trouble was. They reported that it seemed to be a long ridge of stones. A few of the stones appeared to be unusually large, so the team decided to move some of them to one side. When they did, a number of pieces of wood were uncovered.

People in the town said that they looked like bits of a shipwreck. Experts came down from Copenhagen's National Museum. They surprised everyone by saying that the remains were those of a Viking ship. They wanted to see some more of the fragments but it's hard to dig under water.

A metal dam was driven into the sea bed right round the ridge. Then the water was pumped out. By the summer of 1962, the diggers were able to go to work.

In less than five months, tens of thousands

top Parts of Viking ships
above Digging inside the dam

of pieces were rescued. For a while they had to be kept in special tanks. If they had been allowed to dry out, they would have shrunk and twisted. After this they were soaked in chemicals so that they would keep their shape.

It took a while for the chemicals to work but at last the men from the museum could try to fit the pieces together. It was like doing a giant jigsaw puzzle. It will take them years to finish the job. A special display hall has been built in Roskilde so that the public can see the work going on.

Enough has been done already to show that there were five wooden ships. They all date from Viking times and are probably over a thousand years old. No two of them are alike. There was a small ferry or fishing boat. Almost three quarters of this ship has been found. It is nearly forty feet long and eight feet wide.

One of them was a merchant ship which carried cargoes across the North Sea and the Baltic. It is about three and a half feet longer than the ferry. The larger merchantman was built for crossing the Atlantic to Iceland. It measures fifty-two feet from stem to stern.

There were two warships as well. The smaller one is only half complete. Even so, it was sixty feet long when it was first made. The largest one of all was so big that the diggers thought at first it must be two separate vessels. Then they realized that they had found a Viking longship. This was the kind of ship the Vikings used for their greatest voyages. It was the type they chose when they were not just raiding but coming to conquer and settle in new lands.

Most of the ships found once had a mast and sail and also a row of holes in the top planking for the oars to go through. The smallest ship could be managed by only four or five men but the longship carried fifty rowers. It was more than ninety feet long and nearly fifteen feet wide.

All the vessels seem to have been weighted with stones to make them sink. Perhaps the people of Roskilde had tried to block the harbour entrance to keep out raiders.

The ship museum at Roskilde

2 The People

No one knows where the name 'Viking' comes from. It may mean someone who lives by a 'vik', or creek. The word is often used for those people from the northern lands who sailed, raided and traded in ships like the ones found in Denmark. They travelled all over Europe and a good distance outside it as well. Saxons called anyone a Viking, or a Dane, if he had come here to raid or conquer, whether he came from Sweden, Denmark or Norway.

Life was hard in those countries. A lot of the land was mountainous or sandy heathland. None of this is good for farming. The people had a job to grow enough food for themselves. If we take a look at a village we can see something of what their lives were like.

It is a morning in early summer at Tarby. The villagers are busy. Women are washing clothes or making them, preparing meals, carrying water from the stream and doing lots

of other kinds of jobs. It is strange but there don't seem to be very many men about. There are plenty of children but the only men around look rather old.

The reason is that most of the younger men have gone to sea. The fields near the village don't grow very much food so the villagers have to make up the difference with fish. Sometimes they catch a seal; if not, the children gather shellfish and birds' eggs.

One of the children shouts from the beach. The fleet is coming in. Soon they are unloading the catch. Some will be cooked in the long-house kitchen for the feast. This will be done by thralls, as the Vikings call their slaves. The rest of the fish will be cleaned and then salted down or smoked so that it will keep.

When the fishermen have eaten and drunk, the chief tells them that he would like some of them to come on a raiding party with him. The target is a monastery in England.

Einar, one of the warriors, agrees to go in the chief's longship. They will leave in a week's time. Einar decides to take his son Thorkel with him. It will be Thorkel's first raid.

3 Life at Sea

The figurehead of a Viking ship

A week later, the Tarby men are joined by Vikings from three or four other villages. There are to be three longships, two from the villages up the coast and one from Tarby itself. The Vikings are very good boat builders and sailors. They have to be. Those seamen and ships which were not good enough never came back home from fishing or raiding.

Sea Foam is the name of the Tarby boat. It is the largest of the three. It is built of thin, springy oak planks. These overlap slightly and are fastened to the ribs with nails or wooden pegs. Any gaps have been filled in with lengths of tarred wool. The hull is painted all over with tar to keep the water out.

Thorkel and Einar are helping to load the ship with the things they will need. Thorkel is almost a grown man and makes light of the loads. There are barrels of smoked fish and meat, sacks of oats, bags of salt, casks of water, barrels of ale, tents, oars, cooking pots, tools, weapons and armour.

The *Sea Foam* has no cross seats, or thwarts, so each man sits on a chest while he rows. In the chest he will put his own belongings, such as spare clothes, chain mail coat, helmet, sword and axe. Einar and his son do not wear their war things but are dressed in everyday clothes. Each has trousers of animal skin, belted at the waist. Thorkel wears a green woollen tunic while his father's is red. Each has a sleeveless sheepskin jacket with a cloak on top. They have round leather caps. Their boots are also of leather.

The crew say their goodbyes and push the *Sea Foam* into the waves. They scramble aboard. There are forty men in the crew and about thirty in each of the other boats.

The oars are pushed out and the men begin to row. The ship is steered with a large paddle at the stern. The steersman calls out the time so that the men can row together.

The wind is blowing off the shore, so as soon as the ship is far enough out, the oars are pulled in and the single mast hauled up into its place. Then the sail fills with air. The men will not row again until they are near the end of their journey – unless the wind drops or changes direction.

A lot of Viking raiders keep in sight of the coast until they can see England across the Channel. Einar's chief means to go straight across the North Sea.

Vikings know how far north or south they are, even if they haven't seen land for days. They use the sun and the stars to help them. They can also tell the time from the sun and stars to within a quarter of an hour.

The chief divides the crew into two groups. One group cooks some food and then sleeps. The other men bale out water, trim the sail and act as look-outs. They musn't get separated from the other ships. These are not easy to see on a dark night, especially if the weather is bad.

They take it in turns to eat, sleep and be on watch. More than a week goes by before they are in sight of land. One of the crew knows the coastline. They are only five miles from the monastery they are going to attack.

4 A Viking Raid

Sometimes the Vikings take horses with them on a raid. When they beach the ships the horses can get over the low sides and the riders urge them on through the water. The *Sea Foam* doesn't carry horses this time. The raiders are unlikely to do much fighting. Monks don't usually meet them with swords.

When they get to the right place the sail is furled and the mast is lowered. The oars are untied and pushed out. The men row hard for the beach. As the keel grates on the sand, most of them are ready to jump over the side and wade ashore. A few will be left to guard the ship and drive wooden stakes into the sand. The ship will be tied to these to stop it floating away.

The fighting men are now dressed for war. Their round leather caps act as padding for the metal helmet which goes on top. A small piece of iron from the helmet rim protects the eyes and nose. Each man has a thick leather tunic. Those who can afford it have softer leather coats with little iron rings sewn on them. They carry wooden shields with iron edges. Each man has either a sword or a battle axe.

Let's hear from Thorkel what it was like to go on a raid. We'll ask him if his first one was exciting. 'Yes it was,' he says, 'and it might have been more exciting if there had been any berserkers. I looked round to see if there were any as we were trudging up the beach.'

'What are berserkers?' we ask.

'Warriors who work themselves into a rage with oaths, chanting insults until they

are blood mad. From then on, they don't care about their own safety, nor even if they get killed.

'As I say, I looked round but no one was shouting anything. All was quiet except for the waves, the seabirds and the crunch of our feet on the pebbles.

'Then we scrambled up some rocks, over the fields behind and on into the woods, where the chief told us what to do. Once through the belt of trees, there was open farmland in front of the monastery. The chief divided us up into groups and told us to wait when we got to the edge of the wood. I wanted to get a better look and I peered through the bushes.

'One of the monks who was working on the farm must have seen me because he raised the alarm. The monks dropped their spades and hoes, tucked up their robes and ran. There was nothing else to do but give chase. I remember one monk stood his ground with a hoe in his hands. A Viking cut him down with a sword blow and I knew that he was dead.

'I had seen men killed before but not like this. I was half-ashamed and half-excited. I suppose I'd have done the same in his place –

but he shouldn't have got in our way. He wasn't the last monk I saw killed that day, although I think most of them got away.

'I know I stood staring at that first dead body until my father shouted at me. We broke into the buildings and took whatever we could find. The church had the most treasure. There were gold and silver ornaments such as crosses, plates and candle holders. We had sacks to put the things in. Before we left, some of the wilder ones overturned the altar and set fire to it.

'As soon as we were sure there was nothing else worth having, we made our way back to the boats. I expect I'll go on other raids as I get older but I'm sure I'll never forget this one.'

Years later, Thorkel will come back on a different kind of voyage. This time there will be hundreds of longships, not just three. The Vikings will be coming to England, not to steal ornaments but land.

Long after his time, the Vikings from Denmark will have conquered all of northern and eastern England. The country will be divided between the Saxons in Wessex and the Vikings in the Danelaw.

5 The Vikings in Normandy

The Vikings raided, traded and conquered in many places. They settled in the islands to the north and north west of Scotland. They set up trading posts in towns such as Dublin and York. They reached the Mediterranean by travelling along the rivers of Russia. They attacked France, southern Italy and even Africa.

They were so feared that Christians used to end their prayers by saying, 'From the fury of the Northmen, Good Lord deliver us.' Some Christian kings paid them to go away. The money was called Danegeld. Some kings gave them land to settle in, hoping they would drive off any other raiders.

Their manners were rough. A story is told about Rollo the Ganger. Rollo was the leader of a Viking band of warriors. They were allowed to settle in north west France. He was such a tall man that his feet dragged on the ground when he rode his pony. His men said he was 'ganging', or walking.

King Charles of France knew that he was both cruel and proud, so he ordered the

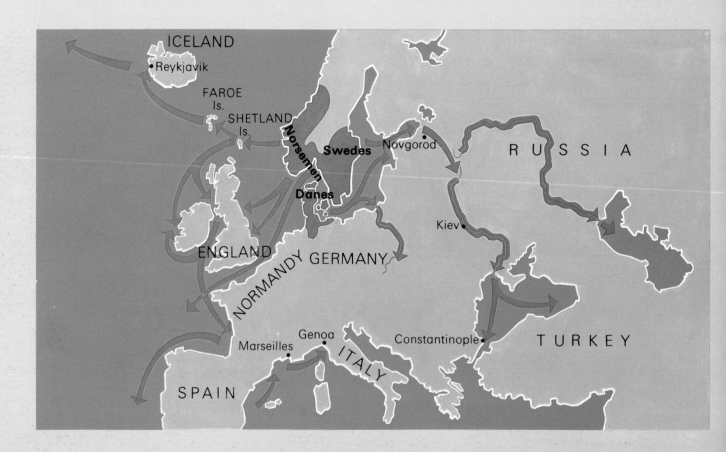

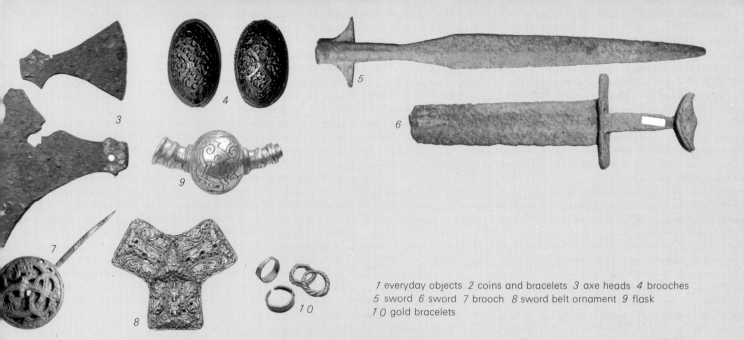

1 everyday objects 2 coins and bracelets 3 axe heads 4 brooches
5 sword 6 sword 7 brooch 8 sword belt ornament 9 flask
10 gold bracelets

Viking to kiss his foot. Rollo bent down and took the king's foot in his hand. Instead of kissing it, he heaved with all his strength. The astonished king flew through the air and landed on his back behind the throne. Rollo had too many Vikings with him to be punished. In fact, he later took the title of Duke.

Because the area he ruled was owned by Northmen, the French called it 'Normandy'. It was from here that the Vikings, or Normans, were at last to launch a successful attack on England.

Not all the Vikings had settled down by this time. Many went on exploring. Some got as far as Baghdad in the Near East, others went in the opposite direction.

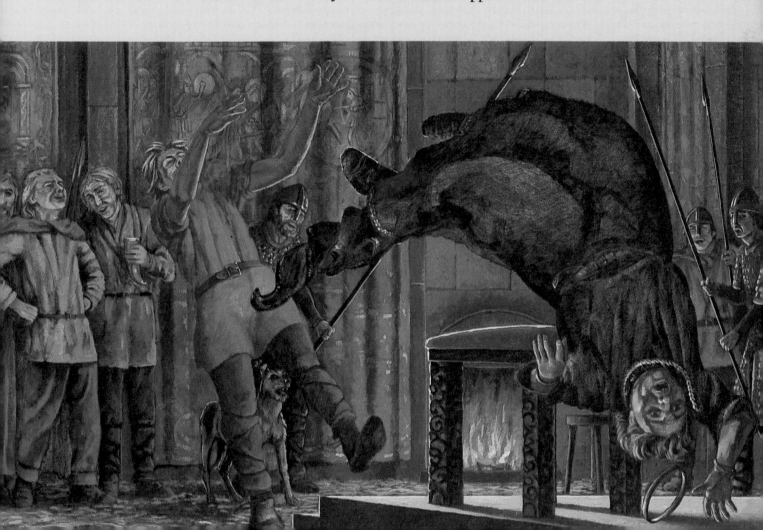

6 Eric the Red

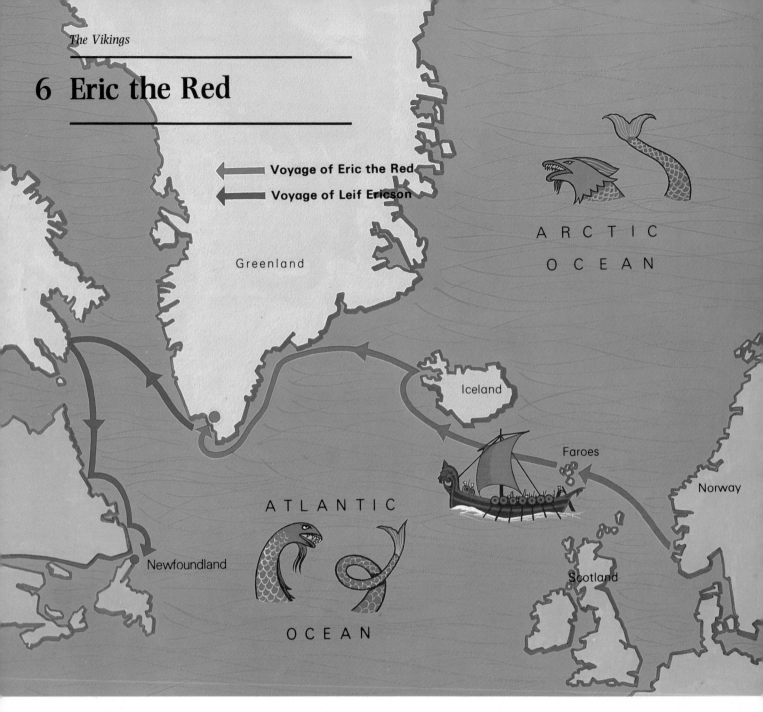

→ Voyage of Eric the Red
→ Voyage of Leif Ericson

ARCTIC OCEAN

Greenland

Iceland

Faroes

Norway

ATLANTIC OCEAN

Newfoundland

Scotland

Perhaps the most surprising voyages were made by Eric the Red and his family. Eric killed a man and was told to leave Norway. He sailed for the Faroe islands and then on to Iceland. Irish monks had discovered Iceland but it was the Vikings who settled there. When Eric landed in 982, he was told of a great land to the west. A sailor named Gunbjørn had once been driven ashore there.

Eric set sail for this new country with his wife and children, plus a few friends. They rowed and sailed westward for several days before sighting land. It didn't look very inviting so they went round the bottom of the island and up the west coast where they landed. Eric called it Greenland.

The country was rather like north Norway but it had no trees. A man called Bjarni tried to bring them a cargo of timber but he was blown off course by a gale lasting several days.

When the weather cleared he saw land. He didn't stop to see what it was. He sailed the hundreds of miles back to Greenland. When he reached Eric's house, he told him what he had seen. Eric's son Leif made up his mind to look for this strange place as soon as he was old enough.

His chance came in the year 1001. He set sail for the west and found Bjarni's land. A landing party explored but there were too many rocks and stones so they sailed south. Twice more they went ashore. Finally they found a good place with trees and grass. They called it Vinland. They built huts and spent the winter there, bringing the timber back to Greenland in the spring.

Other members of Eric's family went to Vinland and tried to make their homes there. They were attacked by the natives and had to leave. Vikings went on trying to live in Vinland for years.

Most of this story was not written down for centuries. When it was, some people said that Vinland must have been America. Others said the story was all lies and the Vikings could never have got so far. In modern times, men

These houses in Iceland today are similar to the ones Eric the Red would have known

have dug up the remains of a blacksmith's forge in Newfoundland. They also found traces of some buildings.

There is no doubt they were the work of Vikings. Nor is there any doubt that men from Europe had landed in America almost five hundred years before Columbus set sail.

Excavation of a Viking site in Newfoundland

7 Saxon and Dane in England

We read earlier how Alfred had beaten the Danes and made them keep to their own part of the country. Unfortunately for the Saxons, Alfred died in the year 901. The Anglo Saxon Chronicle, which he ordered to be kept, gives us many facts from the period. Some of the books which he translated from Latin himself can still be read.

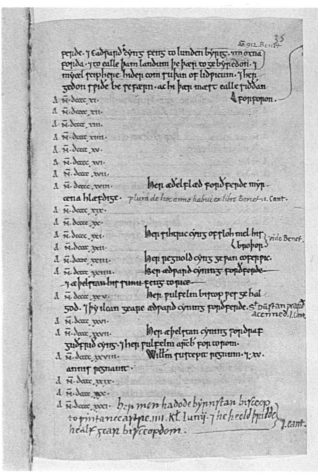

A page from the Anglo-Saxon Chronicle

In the Ashmolean Museum at Oxford is a reminder of the gentler side of King Alfred. It is a beautiful gold brooch with what may be a picture of Alfred himself on it. Around the edge it says, 'AELFRED MEC HEHT GEWYRCAN', which means 'Alfred had me made'.

Alfred was called 'the Great' by his fellow Saxons. This was not only because of his learning but also because he stood up to the Danes. He raised an army which beat them on land and he made an English navy which

Alfred's introduction to a book by Pope Gregory

beat them at sea.

The kings who came after him were not all so good at fighting invaders. Athelstan was the best of them. He was Alfred's grandson and was crowned at Kingston in 925. He called himself 'King of Britain' and he won a great battle against a huge army of Vikings, Scots and Britons at Brunanburh.

No matter how many times the Saxons beat the Danes, they were never able to drive them out completely. Many towns in the north and east of England keep their Danish names to this day. You can be fairly sure a place was once a Danish settlement if its name ends with 'by', 'thwaite', 'thorp' or 'toft'.

In the year 980 a new Danish threat appeared. This time there were not just little groups of raiders but a large army. They had been gathered together in camps in Denmark. Their leaders didn't just want plunder, they had come to conquer the whole country.

The Saxon King Ethelred tried to buy them off with Danegeld. The people of England had to hand over more than 150,000 pounds of silver. It did no good. In 1013 another Danish army arrived. Their leader was Swein Forkbeard. The Danes captured London and Ethelred fled to France. Swein was accepted as king but died shortly afterwards. His son came over to take his place. Ethelred also died, leaving a son named Edmund Ironside to carry on the fight.

Swein's son, whose name was Canute, beat Edmund in East Anglia and became the first Dane to rule the whole of England without argument. He tried to reign as Alfred had done and it seems that the Saxons were willing to have him as king. The Danes still call him 'the Great,' as the Saxons had once called Alfred.

When Canute died, his sons were not nearly such good rulers. The last of them, Hardicanute, left no son to reign in his place. With the help of Earl Godwin, Edward the Confessor became king in 1042. He was another son of Ethelred and therefore a Saxon.

It seemed that the threat of the Norsemen was ended. It was not so. The descendants of Rollo the Ganger in Normandy were already beginning to look at England with greedy eyes. The last great invasion of England by the men from the north was not too far off.

Manuscript illustration of King Canute

8 A Story

Here is a story that the Vikings used to tell about their hero-god, Thor.

He was big and strong. He had a magic belt and a magic hammer. If he pulled the belt tight he became twice as big and twice as strong. His hammer never missed its mark when he threw it and it always came back to his hand. One day Thor was told that there was a land of giants who were much bigger and stronger than he. He thought he would challenge them to see who was the stronger. He set out for giant land with a boy as a servant and a friend named Loki.

When they had been walking for a long while, it grew dark. Thor spotted a great hall in the forest, so they went in through an enormous doorway and lay down to sleep.

In the middle of the night the ground heaved under them. They started to their feet and Thor took up his hammer. 'Quick!' shouted Loki, 'into this small side room. It will be easier to defend if we are attacked.' They stayed on guard all night but nothing happened.

In the morning they found the cause of the noise. It was a giant snoring. They woke him up and he told them his name was Skrymir. Then he asked for his glove back. It was a moment or two before Thor realized that it was the giant's glove in which they had passed the night. The side room was one of the fingers!

Skrymir offered to show them the way and carry their bundles inside his own. When they stopped to rest, the giant fell asleep again but Thor was hungry. Alas! Skrymir had tied the knots on his bundle so tight, Thor could not undo them. He tried to wake the sleeping giant but Skrymir did not stir. Thor shook him and punched him. Then he hit him with his magic hammer. The giant brushed the hammer away, muttering, 'Must have been an insect,' and snored on. Again Thor hit him. 'Must have been a twig dropping,' mumbled Skrymir without waking.

For the third time Thor raised his hammer. Then he brought it down with all his might on the giant's head. Skrymir woke up and said sleepily, 'It's time we were on our way, friend Thor. This place is uncomfortable. An acorn has just dropped on my head.'

When they came to the castle of the king of the giants, Skrymir told Thor to be careful. 'You think I'm a giant,' he said, 'but here I'm just a little one. Farewell, friend Thor.'

The gates were locked but Loki scrambled through the crack under the door, followed by Thor and the boy. The king of the giants was waiting for them. 'Welcome to my home,' he said, 'but you can only stay one night. Of course, you could stay longer if any of you is a champion.' He looked at them. 'What can you do, each of you?' he asked.

The boy said he could run fast but the giant's butler beat him easily. Loki boasted that he could eat more than anyone. The king laughed and ordered a servant to bring a wooden trough of meat. Loki ate his half but the servant ate not only the meat but the bones and the wooden trough as well.

Thor said he would try a drinking contest. The king had a horn brought in and told him that most giants could drain it in one go. Thor found that the level had only fallen an inch after his third swallow. He tried to raise the castle cat off the floor to prove his strength

but could only lift one of its paws.

To cover his shame, he boasted of his skill at wrestling but the giant's old nurse pinned him to the ground.

The next morning the giant king led them to the gate of the castle. 'Don't be downhearted, Thor,' he said. 'Now that you are safely out of my castle, I can tell you that I wouldn't have had you as a guest at all if I'd known how strong you were.'

'Strong?' exclaimed Thor, in surprise. 'You mock me, giant.'

'Indeed not', said the giant. 'I can see I must confess, Thor. I played a trick on you. Several tricks, in fact. I was Skrymir and you very nearly killed me. I put a spell on my bundle. No wonder you could not loosen the knots.

'My butler, the one who outran your boy, was none other than Thought. Nothing is faster than Thought, Thor. Why do you think Loki was outeaten? My servant was Fire

himself in disguise. Fire eats almost as fast as Thought moves.

'Now we come to your part, Thor. When you could not drain the horn, it was because one end of it dipped down into the sea. The levels of the oceans all over the world have dropped because of what you did. The cat you could not lift was the serpent which binds the whole world together.'

'But what about the wrestling?' asked Thor. 'To be beaten by a woman! And such an elderly one!'

The giant laughed so loudly that the stones shook. 'Haven't you guessed? The nurse was Old Age, against whom no one can win.'

Thor smiled for the first time since they had started out. 'Farewell, Thor,' said the giant. 'You did too well! Please don't come back here again!' With that, he slammed the gates shut. Thor laughed and went away with his two companions.

Work Section

Understand your Work

1 Viking Ships
1 Where is Roskilde?
2 What did the divers find?
3 Who identified the remains of the ship?
4 Why was the dam built?
5 Why were the remains kept in special tanks?
6 How old were the ships?
7 What sort of ships were found?
8 Why do we think the ships were sunk by their owners rather than by an enemy?
9 Look at the photographs on page 90. How can you tell that the objects are parts of ships?
10 What does the photograph on page 91 show?

2 The People
1 Where does the word 'Viking' come from?
2 Where did the Vikings come from?
3 What sort of land is no good for farming?
4 List some of the things the villagers eat.
5 Where will the meal be cooked?
6 What is a raiding party?
7 What is a monastery?
8 What is the name of Thorkel's father?
9 Describe what is happening in the picture on pages 92 and 93.
10 What do the houses have instead of chimney pots?

3 Life at Sea
1 How many boats from Tarby take part in the raid?
2 Were the Vikings good boat builders?
3 What sort of wood is the Tarby ship made from?
4 What is a thwart?
5 Where do the men keep their belongings?
6 How many men go on the raid?
7 Do the men have to row the boat all the way?
8 What are the differences between Viking ships and Saxon ships?
9 Look at the picture on page 94. What sort of an animal does the carving represent? Make your own design for a figurehead.
10 Look at the picture on page 95. Which way is the ship moving?

4 A Viking Raid
1 Are there horses on the Tarby ship?
2 Why don't the Vikings expect the people at the monastery to put up much of a fight?
3 What is a keel?
4 Why are wooden stakes driven into the sand?
5 Describe what a Viking wore in battle?
6 What was a berserker?
7 Why did the Vikings attack monasteries?
8 Which parts of England did the Vikings later invade?
9 Make a drawing of the sort of helmet the Vikings are wearing in the picture on pages 96 and 97.
10 Which part of the monastery are the Vikings plundering?

5 The Vikings in Normandy
1 What is a trading post?
2 What is the Mediterranean?
3 What was Danegeld?
4 What does 'ganging' mean?
5 Why do you think King Charles wanted Rollo to kiss his foot?
6 Why couldn't the king punish Rollo?
7 Why did the French call Rollo's lands 'Normandy'?
8 Name some of the places the Vikings visited or conquered.
9 Describe two of the objects on pages 98 and 99. Say what you think they were used for.
10 Try and draw one of the swords or axes showing how it might have looked when it was new.

6 Eric the Red
1 Why did Eric have to leave Norway?
2 Where are the Faroes?
3 Who discovered Iceland?
4 How is Greenland different from Norway?
5 What happened to Bjarni?
6 Why do you think Eric and his men needed the timber?
7 Why didn't Eric and his men cut down timber where they had landed?
8 How do we know the Vikings discovered America?
9 Where is Newfoundland?
10 Look at the photograph of Glaumber farm in Iceland at the top of page 101. Do you think it is very different from the sort of houses the Vikings would have lived in, in Eric the Red's day?

7 Saxon and Dane in England
1 Give another name for the Vikings.
2 What is the Anglo-Saxon Chronicle?
3 Where is the Alfred jewel?
4 What did Alfred do to resist the Danes?
5 Who was Athelstan?
6 Who was the first Dane to rule all of England?
7 Who became king in AD 1042?
8 Who was Rollo the Ganger?
9 Estimate the size of the Alfred jewel.
10 In which language is the Anglo-Saxon Chronicle written?

Use your Imagination

1 Why is it easier to find and excavate the remains of buildings than it is to find and excavate the remains of ships?
2 Which do you think was the most dangerous occupation, fishing or farming?
3 Make a list of the things the Vikings ate. What sorts of things do you eat that they would not have known about?
4 Imagine that you are Thorkel. Write what it felt like to go on a raid.
5 If there had been plenty of good farm land in the Vikings' homeland, do you think they would ever have invaded England?
6 Why do you think the English did not raid the Vikings?
7 What happened to the Saxons when the Vikings started to attack England?
8 Who, do you think, were the natives of Vinland who drove out the Viking settlers?
9 Why do you think story-telling was so important to the Vikings?
10 Why were the monasteries such good places to raid?
11 Imagine you are the chief at the village of Tarby. Write a speech setting out your plan for the raid on the English monastery. What would be the most serious problems and dangers when spending weeks at sea in an open boat?

Further Work

1 In order to get an idea of how big a Viking ship was, make a full-sized outline of one in your playground.
2 What are the main differences between Roman, Saxon, and Viking ships?
3 People used to think that the Vikings wore horns on their helmets. Can you find any reliable evidence to suggest that they did? Would horns have been a help or a hindrance during a battle?
4 Draw a picture of a Viking warrior. Study pictures of clothes and weapons before you make a start.
5 Find out all you can about a Viking settlement. York is a good choice as a good deal of excavation work is still going on there.
6 Find and read as many stories as you can about the Norse gods and heroes. The library will be able to help.
7 A town or a village with a name ending in 'by', 'thwaite', 'thorp', 'toft', or 'garth' was probably once a Viking settlement. List all the ones you know.
8 To get some idea of the problems facing the Roskilde ship restorers, you might try the following experiment. Take three fairly difficult jigsaws and mix them up. Now try to do any one of them.

Chapter Six   The Normans

1 Two Battles

A scene from the Norman invasion of Britain from the Bayeux Tapestry

This is part of a piece of embroidery. It is rather special. To start with, it is over 900 years old. It is called the Bayeux Tapestry.

The Saxon king, Edward the Confessor, had ruled England for nearly a quarter of a century. As he lay dying, he sent for Harold, the son of Earl Godwin. He had enough strength to tell Harold that he was to be the next king. Then he died. Harold was crowned king without delay.

At least two other men thought they should be King of England. One was Harald Hardrada, King of Norway. The second was Duke William of Normandy.

William always said that Edward had promised the English throne to him. He also said that Harold Godwinson had sworn to help him become King of England. It seems likely that Harold was tricked into doing this when he had been shipwrecked in Normandy some years before.

King Harold's brother, Tostig, had been Earl of Northumbria. He was a cruel man and was ordered to give up his earldom and leave the country. He had gone to Norway and urged Hardrada to attack England. If the Norwegians won, he would get his earldom back.

Harold knew there would be an invasion so he got his army ready to beat off the attacks. He didn't know which one would come first. It might be the Norwegians if the wind was from the north. If it was a southerly

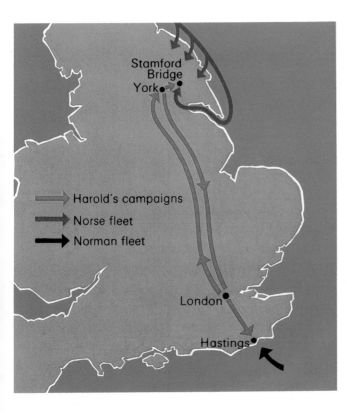

wind then the Normans would win the race.

Harold kept his army near London ready to march north or south. Throughout the summer of 1066 they waited and nothing happened. At last the men grew impatient. They wanted to go home and help gather in the harvest. Harold gave in and let half of them go.

The wind was wrong for Duke William. Day after day it blew steadily from the north, keeping his ships in port. Unluckily for King Harold, it was just right for the Norwegians.

News reached Harold that Hardrada and Tostig had landed in Yorkshire. The message said that there were 300 ships and thousands of Vikings. Harold set off with his army to walk the 180 miles to York, which the Vikings had captured.

When he arrived, a messenger from the Norwegians said that Hardrada demanded the land of England. 'Tell your king,' said Harold, 'he shall have just six feet of our land. For his grave,' he added. Then he said thoughtfully, 'Hardrada is a tall man and his body will not fit a normal grave. You had better offer him seven feet!'

We do not know what Hardrada said when he heard the reply but Harold's words came true. Both Tostig and the Norwegian king were slain in the Battle of Stamford Bridge, which the Saxons won.

Harold had no time to enjoy his victory. News reached him that the wind had changed and that Duke William had landed on the south coast. The Saxons made the long march all the way back again to fight another battle.

Harold put his army of 7,000 men at the top of a slope about seven miles from Hastings. There was a marsh on each side. Harold made some of his men line up across the front of the army with their shields touching. At about nine in the morning, William's archers fired arrows but few of them got past the shields. Then he attacked with men on horseback but still the line held. Every time the Normans came up the hill, the Saxons drove them back with spears, axes and swords.

One group of Norman raiders scattered and some of the Saxons made the mistake of leaving the shield wall to chase them downhill. Norman arrows came flying down over the shields that were left and Norman horsemen poured through the gap. Harold was slain – some say by an arrow in the eye. The fighting went on until it was dark. When it was done, Saxon rule was over for ever.

Battle Abbey

2 A Castle

Before William left Normandy, he had a wooden fort made. His men took it to pieces and carried it in their ships to England. There they rebuilt it. They might have lost the Battle of Hastings and would have wanted somewhere to shelter.

William's knights knew that they would have to have castles too. Their reward for helping the new king was often a piece of land. Although they had won a battle, they had not conquered all of England. Some Saxons would fight to try to stop the Norman knights taking their land. The safest thing for William's men to do was to put up forts straight away.

Of course, it would have been nice to build a big, strong castle out of stone. But this would have taken a long time, perhaps years. Let's imagine how one man, Baron Roger de Lô, solves the problem. Roger wants something that will be ready much more quickly. He looks round his new lands for a small hill.

There isn't one, so he sets his men to work to make one. On top of it they fit together heavy slabs of oak to make a box-shaped fort. Stables and barracks are built at the foot of the motte, as it is called, and the whole thing is enclosed with a stout fence.

A few years later, when things have settled down a bit, Sir Roger wonders what he can do to make his castle stronger. A friend tells him about Maitre Basville, a man skilled in the art of making stone castles. Sir Roger sends for him.

First of all, Maitre Basville wants to know

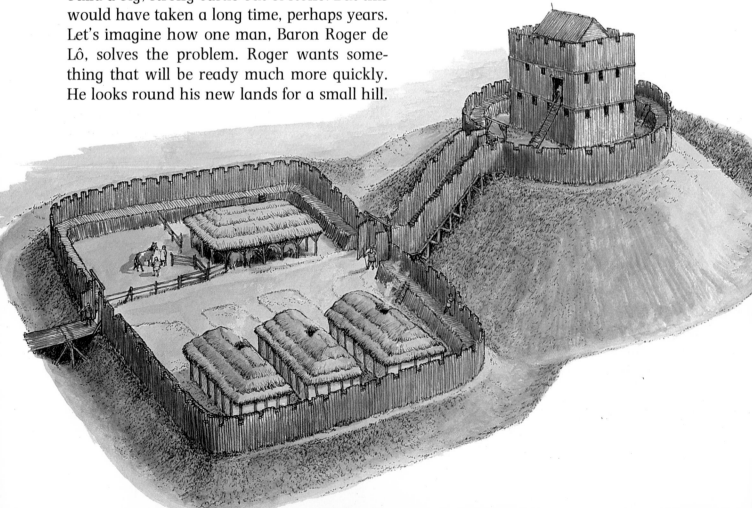

what Sir Roger has in mind and how much he can spend. Sir Roger has large estates and money to spare. They get down to details. The builder tells the Baron not to have a heavy stone building on top of his motte. 'I have seen them,' he says, 'and they are not safe.' They speak in French, for the Vikings of Normandy had long given up their own language.

When they have agreed, Maitre Basville leaves for Normandy. The labourers will be found in England but he has to take on many stone masons, stone cutters, engineers and scaffolders, together with their apprentices. He also has to buy the stone and get it shipped across the Channel to England. Everyone agrees that limestone from Caen in Normandy is the best you can get for castles.

In the meantime, Roger has to get the site ready. It has been decided that the wooden fort must be pulled down but that the new castle should go somewhere else. The builder says there is no longer any need for a motte. Stone castles can be very high, so any flat ground will do.

There is a level place near the bridge over the river. Men on top of a castle roof will be able to stop an enemy crossing the bridge with their arrows. The water from the river can be used to fill the moat.

The chosen place is not empty though. There are several small Saxon houses in the way. This doesn't worry the Baron. He sends his soldiers to turn the peasants out of their homes which are then pulled down. The Saxons are angry but can do nothing.

3 A Baron

Baron Roger de Lô really has only one name. The word 'Baron' is a title. The 'de Lô' part means 'from Lô'. Lô is a town in Normandy. Very few lesser men had more than one name.

Roger is very pleased with his castle. When it is almost complete he walks round it. He sits on a saw bench in the main hall. He and his family have come quite a long way in a short time. His grandfather's grandfather was one of Rollo's Vikings. Before that time, they had scratched a hard living from poor soil. Now he is one of William the Conqueror's trusted men.

Here is a picture of the Baron dressed for war. His helmet has protecting pieces at the front and back like the earlier Viking pattern. He wears a coat of chain mail from neck to knees. It has slits so that he can sit comfortably on his horse. The sleeves are short to leave his arms free to use weapons.

It is a long and difficult job to make a coat of chain mail. The Normans call it a hauberk, which really means 'neck cover'. To start with, that is all it was. Later it became a coat. Some even look like old-time bathing costumes with short arms and legs. All are made of stiff linen or leather. The smith has to make thousands of little iron rings. Some of them are left open so that they can be joined up. Every ring is linked with four others. The rings are fastened to the leather backing. A hood of chain mail goes on Roger's head and his helmet on top of that.

right Falconer from a medieval manuscript
below One type of Norman helmet

Roger's day can be a very long one sometimes. He has to make sure that his officers are doing their jobs properly. They have to see him regularly to let him know what is going on. He has them in one at a time to make their reports.

There are men in charge of collecting rents. Others look after the stables, horses, soldiers, storehouses and the armoury. These are his stewards and bailiffs. Before long he will have to appoint a man to look after the castle. He will be known as the Constable and will tell Roger when repairs are needed or where the defences can be made stronger.

Every now and then he holds a court to try those who have broken his laws. Otherwise he will ride round his estates to make sure that things are going well. If he has nothing else to do he likes to go hunting. Large animals such as deer and wild boar will be hunted with dogs and finished off with spears. He uses a tame falcon to chase smaller game such as hares, rabbits and birds.

4 Life in the Castle

The key for this illustration is on page 116.

DAN ESCOTT

Life in the Castle

The great hall is the most important place in the castle. While all the other rooms in the keep, or donjon, fit between the floors, the hall is two floors high. This is where the main meals are taken. Nearly all those who live in the castle eat together in the hall.

Roger and his wife, the Lady Alicia, sit at the high table which stands on a platform in front of a huge open fireplace. They are warm. So are the important people who are eating at the same table. Those at the far end of the hall can scarcely feel the fire, although they know it is there because the air is full of smoke.

The wooden floor is covered with rushes. There are some bright, coloured hangings on the walls and over the doorways. These help to brighten the greyness which is everywhere. The only light comes from the fire and dozens of rushlights or candles.

The castle is a cold and draughty place. The window spaces have no glass in them. The only way you can keep out most of the rain and snow is to close the wooden shutters. As this also shuts out the daylight, it is only done after sunset.

Although Roger's stewards might buy some of the food they eat, the Baron expects most of it to be grown on his own farms. The Normans don't go shopping for bits and pieces as we do. Everything has to be planned for several months ahead. If things are bought at all, they are bought in bulk.

A lot of food, such as meat and fish, is smoked or salted and packed away by the ton in the storehouses. There has to be enough to go round if there's a siege. By the time the enemy army is camping round your castle, it's too late to think of going out for tomorrow's dinner.

In the summer time there is plenty of fresh food – pork, beef or a little mutton. In the winter, the Baron will get tired of eating meat which has not kept too well. One of the stewards will order his men to go fishing in the river. Some castles have their own ponds which are stocked with live fish.

The salted meat has to be eaten, even if it is going bad. Norman lords often smother it with peppery spices to hide the taste of the meat. Fresh meat is sometimes roasted but more often it is boiled. It is served on stale slices of bread. The leftovers are given to the poor when the meal is over. Roger and his guests drink wine brought over from France. His men have to make do with ale. A cup is filled and passed along the table. Each one takes a sip as it goes by.

The children don't eat with their parents. The boys don't even live with them. At the age of seven or eight, a boy is sent to the castle of a friend or relation to be trained as a knight. In his turn, Roger is training the son of a friend. The boy's name is Hugh. He is about eleven. He passes food to the guests and helps pour out the drinks. As the diners eat mostly with their fingers, Hugh brings them a bowl of water and a towel.

After the fruit and nuts have been eaten, the meal is over. It started at ten in the morning and has lasted well over an hour. It seems rather early to us but everyone has been up since sunrise. Most people sleep in the great hall. They stretch out on the benches or even on the floor, wrapped in woollen cloaks.

Roger and his wife sleep in the solar. This is a small private room above the hall. It has its own fireplace and even a wooden bed screened off with a curtain. Not a lot of hand and face washing is done but Roger has a bath in the solar once a week.

There are lavatories in the corner towers. They are very rough and ready. There is just a wooden seat balanced over a chute leading out to the moat. You have to take a bucket of water with you to flush the toilet.

Lady Alicia spins, weaves and sews for part of the day and so do her two daughters, Adela and Betlindis. The women are expected to make some of the clothes, although the servants do most of the work.

Lady Alicia and her daughters wear the same kind of clothes. They have woollen stockings and soft leather slippers. Alicia wears a slip or undershirt which comes to her feet. A gown goes over this and on top is a cloak or mantle. Her headdress is called a wimple.

In the afternoons, Roger sees to Hugh's training if he has no important business. The boy is taught to use weapons. He can ride already. The second meal is taken at about four or five o'clock. Everyone goes to bed soon after dark.

5 Hugh's Day

1 HUGH RISES EARLY AND, BEFORE BREAKFAST, ASSISTS THE LORD TO BATHE AND DRESS.

2 AFTER A SIMPLE BREAKFAST, HUGH CLEAN AND POLISHES THE LORD'S ARMOUR.

3 HUGH TAKES LESSONS WITH THE PRIES FOR THE REST OF THE MORNING.

5 EVERY DAY HUGH SPENDS SOME TIME AT WEAPON TRAINING.

6 IN THE EVENING HUGH SERVES HIS LOR WITH MEAT AND WINE AT DINNER.

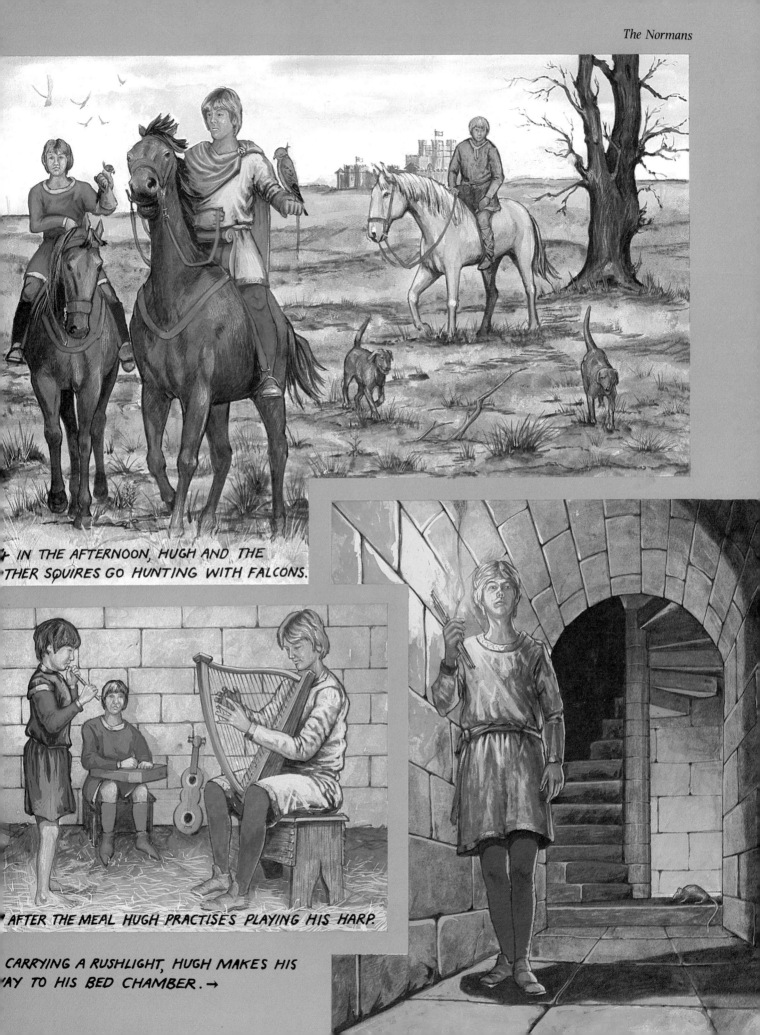

← IN THE AFTERNOON, HUGH AND THE OTHER SQUIRES GO HUNTING WITH FALCONS.

AFTER THE MEAL HUGH PRACTISES PLAYING HIS HARP.

CARRYING A RUSHLIGHT, HUGH MAKES HIS WAY TO HIS BED CHAMBER. →

6 King William and the Feudal System

William said that he owned all the land because he had conquered it. He gave about half of it to those who had fought for him at Hastings. He made sure that the pieces of land were well scattered so that anyone who wanted to rebel against him would find it hard to get an army together.

The men who received land from William were called 'tenants-in-chief'. There were about 200 of them. They were mostly barons, like Roger, but there were also bishops and abbots. The Church was quite a big land-owner. Each tenant-in-chief had tenants of his own. These were the knights, the men who fought on horseback.

All the barons, bishops, abbots and knights were Normans. William made sure that the important jobs went to his own men. Many Saxon earls had been killed in battle but William didn't hesitate to get rid of most of those who were left.

Every knight divided up his land into smaller pieces. These were known as manors. The men who ran them were freemen and a few might be Saxons. Each manor was really a village. The men who actually worked the land were the Saxon peasants. Some were allowed to go on looking after a few strips of land. Others had no land at all. They earned a living by working on someone else's farm.

The feudal system was like a staircase with the king at the top, the tenants-in-chief on the next step down, and so on. Every man had to promise to obey the one above him. This was done at a ceremony. The man who was about to promise knelt in front of his lord. The lord took his hands while the man made the promise.

To pay for his land, each man had not only to swear the oath but, if necessary, to fight for his lord. He might also have to pay rent. Rent was not often paid in the form of money. It was more likely to be some of the things he grew or made. At the very bottom of the system, there were peasants who had to work on the lord's land for three or four days a week. They got no wages for this and had to try to do their own work in the time they had left. In return, the lord swore to protect his peasants from thieves, rebels or any other enemies.

Sometimes there were rebellions. These were usually the work of Saxons, angry at having their land taken from them. Only three years after Hastings, there was an uprising in Yorkshire. Some Danish ships arrived to help the rebels. William sent for his tenants-in-chief and the vassals, as the lesser men were called, to help him. When he had got his men together, he marched north. The Danes sailed for home as soon as they saw the size of William's army. William beat the Saxons and then went on to show them just what any other rebels could expect.

He ordered his men to burn the villages, food stores and haystacks. They drove off or slaughtered all the farm animals. Then the army went back to London.

Those rebels who had not been killed by William's soldiers were faced with starvation in the coming winter. It did not pay to make William the Conqueror angry.

7 The Domesday Book

The Domesday Book is one of the oldest books of its kind in the world. You can go and see it in the Public Records Office in London.

Nowadays, we have to fill in forms for all sorts of reasons. Every ten years there is a census. The head of each household has to say how many people there are living under his roof. To run our country properly, we need to know how many of us there are. This is so that there will be enough schools, roads and hospitals for everyone.

We don't think William I made the Domesday survey just to find out how many people lived in England in 1086. He probably wanted to know exactly what everyone owned so that he could work out what taxes they ought to pay. The year before, William had called his advisers together at Gloucester. He asked them how he could find out what sort of country he ruled and what it was worth.

The advisers worked out a way of doing it. They told the king to send his commissioners to every county in England to ask questions. Let's imagine the scene in a village which is waiting for them to come.

It has been raining hard in Waldham. Now it is only drizzling but the ground is muddy and there are puddles everywhere. The reeve, or headman of the village, is in charge. His name is John. He had been hoping that the meeting could take place out of doors. Now it is raining, they will have to ask their questions inside his house.

'Which people are to be questioned, John?'

'I've been ordered to pick six of the oldest villagers with the best memories. They are waiting next door. I shall be here and so will the priest. In fact, I can see my boy running

towards us. The commissioners must be coming.'

We question the commissioners as they dismount from their horses.

'What exactly are you trying to find out?'

'King William needs to know how much land there is in the village,' replies the elder of the two men. 'Is it good for growing wheat or grazing animals; is it woodland or waste? How much of each kind is there? How many ploughs? Is there a mill? What is it worth? How many pigs, cows and sheep? How many peasants? Who owns what?' 'Don't forget,' says the younger of the commissioners, 'that the jury must tell us more than that.'

'Why do you call them a jury?' we ask. *'And what else can they tell you?'*

'They must all swear to tell the truth and our word for "to swear" or "promise" is "jurer". As to the extra information, we are commanded by the king to ask not only what the village is like now but also what it was like when Edward the Confessor died. That's just over twenty years ago.'

'Won't that lead to arguments? And how are you going to talk to the jury? They can't speak French and you can't speak Saxon.'

Just at that moment the priest arrives and overhears what we are saying. 'I shall translate,' he says. 'The king's men can put their questions. I'll tell the jury what they are and then I'll tell the commissioners what their replies are. Ah! here are the monks. Perhaps you can tell the villagers we're ready.'

Soon everyone is sitting down and candles and rushlights are lit. The questioning goes on for hours. The monks speak French but they write the answers in Latin. 'Every educated man knows Latin,' one of them explains, 'no matter whether he is a Saxon, a Spaniard or a Norman like me. We write with quill pens. They are sharpened with penknives. We sprinkle fine sand over the wet ink to dry it. When every village has been visited, all these papers will be collected and copied on to parchment pages of very large books.'

At last they have finished. The weather isn't any better when they leave. It is still raining.

Although much of England was examined in this way, the work was never properly finished for William I died. It was to be over seven hundred years before England had another survey anything like it.

8 A Story

This is a story which Saxon peasants used to tell about one of their heroes. After the evening meal when they were sitting round the smoky fire, someone would say, 'What about Hereward the Wake?' and then they would all want to talk at once. Everyone has a different story. Quite a lot of the tales have been made up. A few are true but they happened to someone else. This is the story that most of them would agree about.

Hereward, they say, was the son of Earl Leofric of Mercia. His mother was Lady Godiva. When he grew up in Saxon England he rented a great deal of land. Most of it was in south west Lincolnshire and it belonged to the abbeys at Peterborough and Crowland.

Just four years before the Battle of Hastings, Hereward was forced to leave the country. No one seemed to know what he had done. He was abroad for eight years. When he came back, the Normans had already ruled England for four years.

He found that the kind old Abbot of Peterborough had been turned out by King William and that there was a new man in charge. His name was Turold. Turold would not allow Hereward to set foot on his own lands nor would he give him his belongings back. Hereward was thrown out of the abbey.

Promising himself that he would get his own back, he moved off into the countryside. He met two friends from the old days. One complained bitterly about the Normans. The other said that many Saxons had been made outlaws. They wanted to deal the Normans a blow. Would Hereward help them?

When he told them his own story, they took Hereward to their hideout. There were a great number of Saxons there. One of the men told Hereward that they were expecting a messenger from a Viking band. As soon as the man arrived they questioned him.

'We don't want to go back home empty handed,' said the messenger. Hereward asked him if the Vikings would like to attack an abbey as they had done in the old days.

The attack was arranged. The wicked Turold was killed and the Vikings rowed out to sea with their plunder. Hereward and his followers hid themselves on the Isle of Ely. They had chosen a good place. In those days Ely really was an island. There was firm, hard ground in the middle and all around it a maze of marshes and thickets of reeds. You had to be very sure of the paths if you wanted to get there.

A few pathways led to the island but they turned and twisted so much, it was easy to get lost. At times the path was no more than a few stones under the water. A foot on either side of the hidden stones and you could drown. King William sent a troop of soldiers to punish Hereward but they couldn't get to the island. They camped nearby. Next day they split up into small groups to try to find a way through the marshes. Only half of them came back to camp that night.

News of the rebels spread. Other Saxons went to fight alongside Hereward, including Earl Morcar and the Saxon Bishop of Durham. They raided Norman farms and still more Saxons joined them. After a year of these attacks, William himself was forced to lead a large army against the rebels.

The king camped at Cambridge and worked out a plan. His army would move to the edge of the marshes and begin making a causeway of their own to the island. William thought this could be done by ordering his men to drop lumps of stone into the water until there were enough to stand on. Then more lumps were to be dropped beyond where the men were working, and so on. He hoped that there would then be a straight, dry path right over to Ely.

Unluckily for the Normans, there wasn't enough stone to do this so William had to think of something else. It was late summer and the reeds were dry and brown. If the soldiers could start fires in the right places, they might smoke Hereward out. Making sure the wind would carry the flames towards Ely, William's men did as they were told.

Most of the Saxons gave in. They came across the pathways coughing and spluttering and yielded to the king. William was not as pleased as he might have been. Among the prisoners there was no sign of Hereward. The cunning Saxon had somehow managed to escape.

One ending of the story that the peasants told round their fires for years afterwards was happier than what probably happened. It is said that Hereward made his peace with William. Because he had been so brave and such a good fighter, he was allowed some of his land back again. Another ending says he died fighting Normans in France. We just don't know.

Work Section

Understand your Work

1 Two Battles
1 What is the Bayeux Tapestry?
2 Which three men wanted to be King of England when Edward the Confessor died?
3 What was the name of King Harold's brother?
4 Of which country was Harold Hardrada king?
5 Why did King Harold's army want to go home? Did the king let them go?
6 Who fought at the Battle of Stamford Bridge? Who won?
7 Who landed on the south coast while King Harold and his army were in the north?
8 What happened at the Battle of Hastings?
9 Look at the soldiers on the Bayeux Tapestry. Is there much difference between the Saxon and Norman armour?
10 Describe what is happening in the scene from the Bayeux Tapestry.

2 A Castle
1 Why did Duke William bring a portable fort with him when he invaded England?
2 How did William reward the knights who fought with him?
3 Why did William's men build wooden forts rather than stone ones?
4 What is a motte?
5 How long is it before Roger decides to build a stone castle?
6 Where does the stone come from?
7 Why is the new stone castle not built on the motte?
8 Why does Roger choose the site near the bridge?
9 Look at the pictures of Roger's two castles. What are the main differences between them?
10 What is the small round building near the pond in the picture of the stone castle?

3 A Baron
1 How did Roger get his other name?
2 Who was Roger's grandfather's grandfather?
3 Where had Roger's ancestors lived before they moved to Normandy?
4 What is a hauberk?
5 What is chain mail?
6 What do Roger's officers have to do?
7 What is a court?
8 What sort of game does Roger hunt?
9 How is the helmet in the photograph on page 113 different from the type Roger is wearing?
10 What does the picture at the top of page 113 show?

4–5 Life in the Castle/Hugh's Day
1 What is a donjon?
2 Why do you think that there is no glass in the windows?
3 Where does most of the food come from?
4 Why must there always be plenty of food in the castle?
5 What did the Normans use spices for?
6 What happens to a boy when he is seven or eight?
7 What is a solar?
8 Where do the family's clothes come from?
9 Look at the illustration of the castle on pages 114 and 115 and say what you could see from the top of one of the turrets.
10 Look at the pictures on pages 118 and 119 and describe how Hugh spends his day.

6 King William and the Feudal System
1 What did William do with England?
2 Who were the 'tenants-in-chief'?
3 What was a manor?
4 Did the Normans work on farms?
5 How did men pay for their land?
6 What promises did a lord have to make to his peasants?
7 How did King William treat the Saxon rebels?
8 Why was it probable that the rebels would starve in the winter?
9 Say what is happening in the picture on page 121.
10 Look at the picture on page 120. How are the costumes of the men on the bottom rung of the staircase different from those of the men at the top?

7 The Domesday Book
1 Where is the Domesday Book?
2 What is a census?
3 Why did King William have the Domesday Book made?
4 What is a commissioner?
5 Who answers the commissioners' questions in each village?
6 What is a juror?
7 In which language is the Domesday Book written?
8 What do the monks use instead of blotting paper?
9 Look at the picture on page 123. What writing implements are the monks using?
10 Why do you think the soldiers are there?